Starting a Digitization Center

Starting a Digitization Center

COKIE G. ANDERSON AND
DAVID C. MAXWELL

Chandos Publishing
Oxford · England · New Hampshire · USA

Chandos Publishing (Oxford) Limited
Chandos House
5 & 6 Steadys Lane
Stanton Harcourt
Oxford OX29 5RL
UK
Tel: +44 (0) 1865 884447 Fax: +44 (0) 1865 884448
Email: info@chandospublishing.com
www.library-chandospublishing.com

Chandos Publishing USA
3 Front Street, Suite 331
PO Box 338
Rollinsford, NH 03869
USA
Tel: 603 749 9171 Fax: 603 749 6155
Email: BizBks@aol.com

First published in Great Britain in 2004

ISBN:
1 84334 073 9 (paperback)
1 84334 074 7 (hardback)

© C.G. Anderson and D.C. Maxwell, 2004

British Library Cataloguing-in-Publication Data.
A catalogue record for this book is available from the British Library.

Typeset by Monolith – www.monolith.uk.com
Printed in the UK by 4Edge Limited - www.4edge.co.uk

Contents

Acknowledgements

The authors would like to thank Kari Scott for her excellent help with editing and suggestions as we moved the book along.

The authors would also like to thank the Oklahoma State University Library faculty and staff for their support in our endeavors, especially Sheila Johnson and Jennifer Paustenbaugh.

About the authors

Cokie G. Anderson received her Masters in Library and Information Studies from the University of Oklahoma. She has been an Assistant Professor at Oklahoma State University since 2000, and directs the OSU Library's Electronic Publishing Center. She is one of the founders and directors of <OKDIGITAL> Association, an Oklahoma non-profit corporation whose mission is to promote digitization in Oklahoma, to provide a forum for discussion of digitization issues, and to foster digital collaboration between institutions.

The author may be contacted at:

cokieanderson@yahoo.com

David C. Maxwell is the Coordinator of Electronic Publishing at the Oklahoma State University Library. David received his BA in Technical Communication from Oklahoma State University in 2001. David has over ten years of computer experience and works extensively with hardware and software.

The author may be contacted at:

pippielouise@yahoo.com

Introduction

One of the great boons of the Web is the online availability of the treasures of the world's libraries and museums. Great paintings, personal letters, diaries of the famous and infamous, ancient papyri, important national documents – all are there for any student with a computer and Internet access. One can read text of the Magna Carta and see images of the original on the British Library's website, view the diaries of George Washington at the Library of Congress, browse Duke University's Papyrus Archive, and download an early American novel from the University of Virginia. Barriers to access have been removed, and the cultural record is available to searchers anytime, anywhere.

Why digitize?

Digitization has benefits beyond improved accessibility. By protecting originals from excessive handling and repeated copying, digitization can be an important component of an institution's preservation strategy. Cooperation between institutions can lead to the reunification of dispersed collections, providing both a convenience to the user and a more complete picture of the person or event memorialized in the collections. A digitized object may reveal information not readily available from the original. When the Nebraska

Historical Society began digitizing photographs of nineteenth-century Nebraska settlers, they used image manipulation software to improve the light and dark tones in the digital images. Suddenly, details not seen in the prints were visible. Instead of merely showing a family standing outside the open front door of their sod cabin, the images now revealed the interior of the house that was previously hidden in shadow. For the first time historians learned that beds were situated immediately inside the door of the cabin to catch any available breeze. Quilts on the beds indicated by their patterns the ethnic and geographic origins of their owners. The photographic collection became an even more valuable source of information once it was digitized. (For more information on the project and to view the enhanced photographs, go to *http://www.nebraskahistory.org/lib-arch/research/photos/digital/history.htm.*)

Deciding to digitize

Digitization is an expensive and time-consuming process, and we will never be able to digitize all the important cultural records in our collections. There is simply not enough time, money and manpower to put everything we would like to digitize online; therefore, we must be extremely selective. You must consider three factors when selecting items for digitization:

- the uniqueness of the materials;
- the demand for them;
- their physical fragility.

One-of-a-kind materials such as manuscripts, personal papers, recordings, artwork or historical artifacts are by their nature prime candidates for digitization. Providing online access is especially important if the material is only available at one location in the world. A digital version will be a great service to users, and it will protect unique materials from excessive handling. Materials that are much in demand will also be given priority for digitization for the same reasons of access and preservation. The making of a digital surrogate may be part of the preservation strategy for fragile materials. All these factors have to be weighed in making your selections. A digitization policy is a good way to formalize selection criteria and to cover issues that arise during any digitization project.

Formulating a digitization policy

The first step in deciding to digitize is formulating a digitization policy. This acts as the equivalent of a collection development policy for your digital collections. It should spell out the requirements a collection must meet in order to be considered for digitization. You may want to begin with a vision statement for digitization that is based on the mission statement of your institution. For example, the Oklahoma State University Library Electronic Publishing Center has the following vision statement:

> The OSU Library participates in the creation and maintenance of the emerging global digital library by digitizing and sharing electronic information. The OSU

Library Electronic Publishing Center, founded in 1996, will pursue this vision by expanding and enhancing access to published and unpublished materials of potential interest to the academic community and general public, especially those unique to OSU or the State of Oklahoma.

This complements the mission statement of the OSU Libraries:

The Library is the central depository of the universe of knowledge for all students and faculty of Oklahoma State University. Its primary mission is to serve as the 'intellectual commons' of the University, providing high-quality resources, services, and gateways to information to meet the needs of OSU's diverse instructional, research, and outreach programs. The Library's secondary mission is that of an information resource for all the citizens of Oklahoma through both direct access to its extensive collections and special services and by sharing these resources as needed with other libraries in the state.

It is important that any digitization effort fits into the institution's overall mission if it is to have the ongoing support of the administration. Once the vision has been stated, the policy should go on to address:

- access;
- the condition of the materials;
- preservation issues;

- the audience for the materials;
- the ownership of rights;
- project support.

Access

The number one reason for digitizing materials is to improve accessibility. Some materials are not accessed because the potential users are unaware of them. Others are held in institutions that are far from major metropolitan areas. Sometimes the materials themselves are so fragile that access to them must be severely restricted. Digitization can address all of these barriers to access. Putting materials online increases public awareness of an institution's holdings and may lead to increased traffic at the museum or library. Distance and travel are no barrier to accessing online collections. As long as users have access to the Internet, they can do their research from anywhere in the world. For professional researchers, this replaces lengthy correspondence with archivists and allows preliminary research to be conducted before traveling to an institution to view original materials. For the younger student or the hobbyist, online collections provide access to materials they would otherwise never get to see.

While enhancing access may be the main goal, a policy must also cover any restrictions on access. This can range from inserting watermarks in photographs to prevent image theft to restricting access only to subscribers, members, or students/faculty. Restrictions on access may be necessary due to ownership rights or copyright issues, or out of the need to recoup costs by charging for access. The latter is not an ideal situation; librarians have a strong tradition of providing free access to all. Sadly, the economic realities may dictate that the price of digitization, including the often overlooked costs of maintaining a digital collection, be subsidized in some way by users. Whatever the institution decides about these issues should be spelled out clearly in the digitization policy.

Condition of materials

A primary consideration is the condition of the original materials. While you may want to give priority to materials that are quickly deteriorating, you must consider the difficulties posed when working with fragile materials. Will the digitization process cause irreparable damage to the originals? In most cases, you do not want to destroy or damage the original to obtain a digital surrogate. If the materials are not unique, you may decide to risk ruining one copy in order to digitize the work, but a unique artifact must never be damaged in the digitization process. The point of digitization is to improve access to the object and to prevent wear and tear on the original, not to replace the original with a digital substitute. Getting a good digital image from an old document is difficult, and enhancing the images or retyping text adds considerably to the cost of a project. If funds are limited, it may be wiser to undertake a project that will require less time and effort to get a usable product.

Preservation

Digitization offers an excellent opportunity to handle conservation and preservation needs. The materials must be in the best possible condition before digitization begins. Make any necessary repairs to minimize damage and produce the best possible digital image. Set out the guidelines for preservation of originals in your digitization policy.

The other preservation issue that must be addressed in your policy is the long-term maintenance of the digital files. Consider how to migrate your files to new hardware and new platforms, how to maintain the functionality of your digital collection, and how to pay for its preservation. All too often projects focus on creating digital text and images and getting the collection online, but fail to plan for the future. If you are investing time, money, and effort in building your digital collection, you want to make sure that it is accessible over the long term. Your digitization policy should include your plans for maintaining your digital files.

Audience

Audience is a key consideration in planning your digital collection. Before you digitize anything, you must know who your audience is. Would the audience be different if the materials were freely available online? Your current audience greatly influences the selection of materials to digitize because it makes sense to give priority to digitizing materials for which there is a high demand. You want to save such materials from the effects of frequent use, and make them easily available to researchers. The potential online audience may lead you to consider documents that are not in high demand, simply because no one knows about them. Think about the hidden treasures of your collection. Perhaps a digital project is the way to reveal them to the world.

Although the Internet has a global audience, you should give greater weight to the interests and needs of the audience in your traditional service area. If your institution has a mandate to serve a particular population, take the wants and needs of that group into account. You may want to concentrate on materials indigenous to your state or country, or of special interest to its citizens. This is the strategy adopted by the OSU Electronic Publishing Center, where materials by or about Oklahomans are given primacy. This not only serves the citizens of our state, but promotes our state and its contributions to users around the world. A thorough knowledge of your current and potential audience is essential to the success of your digital projects. Grant-funding agencies expect you to discuss your stakeholders, i.e. those who will benefit from your project, in any application for funding. Knowing whom you serve and what materials they want to access is critical to your success. Do your audience analysis early, and keep it in mind through all stages of your project.

Ownership rights

The most important issue affecting what you put online is ownership. If you don't have the rights to materials, you can't put them online unless you want ugly and expensive legal problems. If you are dealing with previously published materials, copyright issues come into play. If the material in question is still covered by copyright, you must obtain permission of the copyright holder before you can publish an online version. The copyright holder's willingness to grant permission hinges on whether or not the material still has commercial value. A professional society may be reluctant to allow the digitization of recent issues of its journals which it still hopes to sell, but will permit you to publish online versions of older issues.

It will sometimes be difficult to determine who holds the copyright to a work. This is especially true in the case of newspaper and journal articles. The copyright holder may be the publisher, or it may be the author of the piece. In the latter case, you would have to track down the writer or his or her heirs to obtain a release. These complications can be a deterrent to digitizing previously published material, unless it is old or a government publication. Materials published by government agencies are, in most countries, automatically in the public domain.

Copyright is a complex subject, and any detailed discussion is beyond the scope of this book. The consequences of copyright violations can be severe, and you would do well to consult legal counsel before proceeding if you are in any doubt as to the copyright status of a work you plan to digitize.

Unpublished works, such as personal papers or oral histories, present another set of problems. If the owner of the papers is long dead, there should be few problems with proceeding to digitize. However, if the owner is alive or only recently deceased, the issue is murkier. The owner's permission may be easily obtained, or may have been included in the donor's agreement when the papers were given to the institution. The papers are likely to include letters or other writings to or about other people, some of whom may still be alive. While your institution may have a legal right to publish these letters or documents, there are ethical questions that come into play. If there are derogatory comments or unsavory revelations in the materials that may cause pain or embarrassment to the living, should these documents be made public? What is the institution's responsibility in this case? Similarly, oral histories and interviews may have been recorded before the issue of digitization arose. The interviewee may have misgivings or objections to having their words shared with the world. That is a level of exposure far beyond what they anticipated when they agreed to speak. Unless the subject gave permission for online dissemination at the time of the interview, the appropriate thing to do is to contact them and request permission before making the interview or a transcript available online. It will be helpful to address these matters in a digitization policy, so you have some guidance when such a situation arises.

Project support

Finally, we come to the sine qua non: support, in terms of money and commitment. As we have stated, digitization is an expensive process, and nothing can be done without sufficient funds. The price of digitization includes not only the start-up costs – housing, hardware, software, training – but the labor or outsourcing costs for performing the work of digitization and the ongoing, long-term costs of preservation and maintenance. Your digitization policy should set out guidelines to help you determine costs that require outside funding of some sort and overhead costs that are absorbed into the institutional budget. It should also articulate the institution's commitment to digitization as part of its mission. A digitization program requires a serious, ongoing commitment from the institution to insure its long-term survival. It would be most unfortunate to spend large amounts of time and money digitizing materials that will disappear in a few years because there was no institutional support for migrating and maintaining those digital collections. If an institution is not committed for the long haul, it should reconsider whether it wants to proceed with a digital project.

Selection criteria

Once you have completed a digitization policy, you can use it as a guide for the selection criteria for your digital projects. It can be very helpful to prepare a checklist of these criteria to apply to any proposed project. The OSU Electronic Publishing Center has an online form that allows users to suggest a collection for digitization. The questions asked on this form are based on the selection criteria we have established. The form is available online at *http://digital.library.okstate.edu/ suggest.html.* Stuart Lee of Oxford University has developed a Decision Matrix for Proposed Digitization Projects that is an excellent guide for formulating your selection criteria checklist. It is online at *http://www.bodley.ox.ac.uk/scoping/report.html*.

Summary and resources

This chapter covers the issues to consider before you begin a digitization project.

- Digitization has many benefits: improved access to materials, preservation of originals, promotion of collections, and information revealed by enhanced digital images.

- Digitization is expensive, and we must select materials to be digitized carefully.

- Factors to consider when deciding what to digitize are the uniqueness of the materials, the demand for the materials, and the physical condition of the materials.

- Write a digitization policy before undertaking any digital projects. Sample digitization policies are online. See the National Library of Australia Digitisation Policy at *http://www.nla.gov.au/policy/digitisation.html* and the Digital Library of Georgia Collection Development Policy at *http://dlg.galileo.usg.edu/colldev.html*.

- The digitization policy contains guidelines for access to materials, an analysis of your audience, a plan for preserving original and digital files, a prescription for handling ownership rights issues, a commitment of support for digital projects, and selection criteria for choosing materials to digitize.

■ Examples of selection criteria checklists are online at the Oklahoma State University Library Electronic Publishing Center, *http://digital.library.okstate.edu/suggest.html*, and at Oxford University, *http://www.bodley.ox.ac.uk/scoping/ report.html*.

2

Getting started

Housing

A digitization center may be nothing more than a workstation and a scanner housed in a corner of the library, or it may be a state-of-the-art establishment with digital cameras, lighting, book cradles, oversize scanners, and multiple computers. If you are starting small, a quiet area of your building will suffice, as long as there are sufficient electrical outlets and network connections. If possible, you should choose an area where there is room for expansion. Often you have no choice; you go where there is space available. Try to avoid high traffic areas. Your workspace should be removed from public areas of the institution to allow workers the quiet they need to concentrate on their work. You must be able to secure the area to protect your equipment and the materials you are digitizing.

Physical layout

Having enough electrical outlets and network connections is critical. Take into account printers and scanners, as well as computers. Allow five to six feet (approximately two meters) for each workstation, which is enough room for a scanner, a computer CPU and monitor, and desk space workers can use.

If there is a printer attached to the workstation, allow additional room. If there is no scanner attached, three feet (one meter) should allow sufficient space for a computer. A table provides an area for organizing and preparing materials to be digitized. Shelving keeps materials in order and out of the way. Library book carts can do double duty storing and moving materials. You must decide if you want to use cubicles or movable dividers in the work area. We prefer to keep our area open, as this facilitates workflow and communication in our office.

Lighting

Lighting is an important consideration for a digitization center. Harsh overhead fluorescent lighting causes glare on computer screens, but is almost unavoidable in the modern workplace. The best solution is to remove all of the light bulbs of fixtures that are directly above workstations, and half of the bulbs in the rest of the fixtures in the room. If additional lighting is needed, use desktop or floor lamps with incandescent bulbs. If there are windows in the office area, make sure that they are covered with blinds or curtains that will keep sunlight from causing reflections on computer monitors. Manipulation of images, proofreading online documents, and writing XML code require close attention to detail. Proper lighting will prevent mistakes caused by worker fatigue and eyestrain.

Personnel

The number of persons working in a digitization center varies widely from institution to institution. A university may have two or three full-time professionals and student assistants to help with scanning, proofreading, and encoding tasks. A small organization may only be able to devote one employee part-time to digitization tasks. It is possible to undertake digital projects in either situation, but the number of employees will obviously affect the amount of work output.

The staff for a digital project consists of a project director, an operations manager and project participants. The project director (sometimes called the principal investigator) develops the proposal and evaluation for the project, plans all phases of the project, and estimates costs. The operations manager designs the workflow, establishes standards, prepares materials to be digitized, sets quality control procedures, supervises staff, and handles vendor relations. The project participants actually perform the hands-on work of digitization, i.e. scanning, OCR, image manipulation, XML encoding, and database input. One person could handle all of these responsibilities on a small project. You can outsource some of the work to vendors, and there are some situations, such as rekeying a lengthy text, where this will be the best option. It is also possible for two or more institutions to collaborate on a project and share personnel. We will explore that possibility further in a later chapter.

Training

Training is an essential part of developing your skills and knowledge. Knowing which formats to use for your projects, the software programs needed to perform the work, and attending conferences to network and learn from the experts provides you with excellent resources and valuable information.

Courses and conferences

There are a number of excellent digitization training opportunities in Europe and North America. The Humanities Advanced Technology and Information Institute (HATII) at the University of Glasgow (*http://www.hatii.arts.gla.ac.uk/*) offers a week-long Digitisation Summer School annually. It also has degree programs in digital management and preservation. The University College London School of Library, Archives, and Information Studies (*http://www.ucl .ac.uk/admission/gsp/current/study/depts/art/library.html*) offers a degree in Electronic Communication and Publishing. The Text Encoding Initiative has online tutorials on text encoding in a number of languages at *http://www.tei-c.org .uk/Tutorials/index.html*. The Rare Book School at the University of Virginia (*http://www.virginia.edu/oldbooks/*) teaches courses in electronic texts and images and Encoded Archival Description several times a year. A course in creating electronic text and images is also available at the University of New Brunswick Electronic Text Centre, (*http://www.lib.unb.ca/Texts/*) each August. The Northeast Document Conservation Center (*http://www.nedcc.org/*) offers online courses and hosts the annual School for Scanning at various locations around the US. In the western United States, the Colorado Digitization Project, (*http:// www.cdpheritage.org/*) and Amigos Library Services (*http:// www.amigos.org*) hold regional workshops on digitization topics. Cornell University has put its popular *Moving*

Theory into Practice Digital Imaging Tutorial online in English, Spanish, and French versions (*http://www.library.cornell.edu/preservation/tutorial/*).

The annual conferences of several professional organizations will have sessions and pre-conference workshops on digitization issues. The Association for Computing and the Humanities (ACH) (*http://www.ach.org*), the American Society for Information Science and Technology (*http://www.asis.org*), and the Society of American Archivists (*http://www.archivists.org*) are worth exploring. ACH annual meetings alternate between North America and Europe. Other conferences of interest are Internet Librarian International (*http://www.internet-librarian.com/*) which is usually held in the UK, and Extreme Markup Languages (*http://www.extrememarkup.com/*) which is held each August in Montreal, Canada.

Staff training

You will need to provide training for students and staff in the various tasks of digitization. To simplify this process, prepare step-by-step guides. You can use these help sheets to walk workers through the tasks during training sessions and give them to your staff to use as reference guides. The OSU Library Electronic Publishing Center Operations Manual is an example of such a training tool. It is available online at *http://digital.library.okstate.edu/manual/index.html*. The Text Encoding Initiative has links to Guides to Local Practice (*http://www.tei-c.org/Tutorials/index.html*), prepared by various institutions to assist their workers.

Summary and resources

Housing

- Choose a quiet area. Allow 5–6 feet (2 meters) per workstation (computer and scanner). Make sure you have adequate electrical outlets and network connections.
- Lighting is critical. Avoid overhead fluorescent lighting if possible, and if not, remove some of the light bulbs over computer workstations. Use curtains or blinds to block glare from windows.

Personnel

- A project director or principal investigator develops proposals, plans and oversees projects, and estimates costs.
- An operations manager designs the workflow, prepares materials, and supervises staff.
- Project participants do the actual work of digitization.
- One or two people may perform all of these functions. The larger the staff, the more you can accomplish. Institutions may collaborate on a project and share staff.

Training

- Programs offering hands-on training seminars each summer:
  - HATII at the University of Glasgow (*http://www.hatii .arts.gla.ac.uk/*);

- Rare Book School at the University of Virginia (*http://www.virginia.edu/oldbooks/*);
- University of New Brunswick, (*http://www.lib.unb.ca/Texts/*).

■ Degree programs:
  - HATII at the University of Glasgow (*http://www.hatii.arts.gla.ac.uk/*);

■ University College London School of Library, Archives, and Information Studies (*http://www.ucl.ac.uk/admission/gsp/current/study/depts/art/library.html*).

■ Online resources:
  - Text Encoding Initiative (TEI) Tutorials and Guides to Local Practice (*http://www.tei-c.org.uk/Tutorials/index.html*);
  - Cornell University, *Moving Theory into Practice* (*http://www.library.cornell.edu/preservation/tutorial/*);
  - the OSU Library Electronic Publishing Center Operations Manual (*http://digital.library.okstate.edu/manual/index.html*).

3

Hardware

When starting a digitization center, there are two items you cannot live without: a computer and a scanner. Acquiring the right hardware is one of the most important tasks in building a digitization center. Purchasing quality products that are also cost effective might seem like a big challenge, but with a little time and research can prove rewarding. One of the first decisions in creating the infrastructure of your digitization center is which computer platform you want to use. Currently, the Oklahoma State University Library Electronic Publishing Center uses PCs running Microsoft® Windows® operating systems. Digitization functions perform well on the Apple® Macintosh®, and/or other platforms and operating systems; however, we do not use other formats and do not discuss anything besides PC- and Windows-compatible hardware and software in this book. In addition, the programs, tools, and methods discussed here are what we employ to create our publications.

When looking for the right hardware for your needs, ask yourself these questions:

- How much money is allowed for purchases?
- What equipment is absolutely necessary?
- Where can the equipment be purchased?

Knowing how much money is budgeted can greatly affect the outcome of purchasing equipment. Instead of purchasing only 11 × 17 scanners, you would have to settle for one 11 × 17 scanner and a few 8½ × 14 scanners. Make sure you only purchase equipment that is absolutely necessary – unnecessary extras can waste valuable funds. Knowing what companies are reputable and price competitive makes all the difference when shopping for hardware. Once you have answered these questions, you are ready to take your first steps toward making your digitization center a reality.

Purchasing a computer

The first thing to know before buying a computer is what primary function it needs to perform. Once you have determined the need, you can begin customizing your machines. There are many companies and options to consider when purchasing a computer, and it is generally not a good idea to buy a computer that you cannot fully customize. When you are able to choose what components and how much or little of something you need, you know exactly what you are getting and what to expect from the components you selected. Most computers in retail stores are not customizable and are sold pre-packaged. Therefore, if you needed a different part or more or less of another part, you would have to purchase the extra parts and install them yourself, or remove or replace a component that you could have specified to already be in the machine. The best idea is to find a company or store that allows you to select the components you want in your computer and offers different choices on each component. Many online retailers offer great computers at competitive prices, and you can custom build your computer online to suit your specific needs.

After you determine where you want to purchase your computer, you need to choose the model you feel will do the best job. The easiest way to determine this is to know exactly what components you need, and what systems are currently available that use the technology. The following is a list of the six main parts you need to be concerned with most:

- the processor
- the memory
- the hard drive
- the monitor
- the video card
- the optical drive.

Processor

The processor is one of the most important components of the computer; it determines how fast it can handle the input and send the information back to you. Most computers today are built using the Intel® Pentium® processor; however, the AMD™ Athlon™ is comparable to the Pentium. Intel also offers the Celeron®, which is not as robust as a Pentium-class processor. Our computers use the Pentium processor, so we are using it as a guide in this book. Currently, a Pentium 4 processor that runs at 2.0 GHz or higher is sufficient to run all digitization functions.

Memory

The more memory you have, the better your computer performs. It is always a good idea to add extra memory to enhance the performance of your computer. The minimum amount you should consider is 512 MB, but make sure you can add more in the future to keep your equipment running smoothly and longer. We strongly recommend 1,024 MB, however. Instead of buying a faster processor, you might consider stepping down a few speeds to add more memory, which provides a faster overall performance.

Hard drive

A large hard drive is also important. It helps you store all the necessary information from your operating system to the files you create for digitization. You should plan on having a separate drive (server) dedicated to storing all your files, but you should also have a hard drive on your local computer that can handle the bulk of the files you are creating, and could serve as a backup storage facility if needed. Image files are large, and when scanning several images, you have the potential of losing valuable hard drive space. Most hard drives now are between 40 GB and 250 GB.

Hard drives have also come down considerably in price, so the difference between an 80 GB drive and 160 GB drive is minimal. Doubling the size of your hard drive is worth the cost of a few extra dollars. Think of it this way: you can never have too much hard drive space.

Monitor

A nice large screen is preferable when spending long hours in front of the computer. Digitization requires long hours of looking at the screen, so you should have a monitor that makes it as easy on your eyes as possible. The more space you have, the more you will be able to see onscreen. The ideal size is at least an 18" viewable screen, but the resolution you set your monitor to can also determine how much you can view on the screen. If you have an 18" monitor, but the text and images appear too large, you need to adjust the resolution in the display properties to acquire the right balance of space and comfort to your eyes. The ideal resolution for an 18" monitor would be $1{,}280 \times 1{,}024$ pixels. This setting allows you to maximize your screen size; however, some people might not like the smaller text and images. In this case, you would want to set your resolution to a lower setting.

Since you will be looking at mostly text, you need to be able to see as much of the text as possible. A larger monitor provides this capability. Ideally, you want to have enough viewing area on your monitor to see two areas of text side by side, so you can use your text editing tools efficiently and accurately.

Choosing the right monitor does not have to be a labor-intensive chore, but knowing exactly what you need gives you the ability to make a well-informed decision. The following is a list of some of the major differences between the newer LCD flat panel monitors and the older CRT monitors. There are only a few differences, but these differences are worth mentioning so you can make an informed decision before purchasing:

- LCD monitors require less energy than CRT monitors.

- LCD monitors use less space than CRT monitors.

- LCD monitors generally provide a brighter, sharper screen.

- LCD monitors are free from flicker and easier on the eyes than CRT monitors.

- LCD monitors have fewer problems with glare than CRT monitors and can be effectively used in brightly lit areas.

- LCD monitors are more expensive than CRT monitors.

- LCD monitors are blurry at lower resolutions.

- CRT monitors represent color better than LCD monitors.

- CRT monitors produce better image quality than LCD monitors.

- CRT monitors handle moving images better than LCD monitors because of a better response time and are better suited for video editing.

Currently, the computer industry is continuing to improve the technology in the LCD monitor, and should have the resolution, color representation, and response time issues solved and implemented in the near future. Until then, both types of monitors provide a good solution, but you need to base your decision on which type of monitor is best suited for your center's specific needs and what you can afford.

Video card

The video card and monitor work seamlessly together, but we wanted to separate them into two different categories because they are two entirely different components. The video card is where you plug your monitor into the computer. Having a good card makes all the difference on how well your monitor displays the text and images onscreen. The majority of video cards work fine with most monitors, but newer LCD flat panel monitors with a digital interface use the newer DVI (digital video input) port on the video cards. The older CRT monitors plugged into the VGA connection on the video card and you adjusted your resolution based on the video card's capabilities and your monitor size and preferred resolution.

At present, there are two types of monitors and interfaces for video cards: the older analog CRT monitor, which uses the VGA input, and the newer digital LCD flat panel display monitor, which uses the VGA input and/or the newer DVI to connect the monitor to the video card. Older cards have the VGA-only input, but the newer video cards have both a VGA and DVI input. Depending on what type of monitor you have, it is best to use CRT monitors with the VGA input; however, you can use them via the DVI port with a converter. LCD monitors mostly connect to the DVI port on the computer, but some LCD monitors have both digital and analog ports, while some have only digital and others only analog. You could use either interface depending on whether or not you have a video card that supports either interface or only one, and a converter can always be used if needed. Eventually, all video cards and monitors will use the DVI port to connect to each other.

Optical drive

Optical drives are better known as CD and/or DVD drives. These drives have become an increasingly important part of the computer, especially with the capabilities of recording information to CDs and DVDs for several different purposes.

Most computers today come standard with CD-RW drives and/or a DVD-ROM drive. The majority of CD recording today is done with the CD-R/RW drive and format. CD-R/RW means you can use two types of disks and/or formats in recording: a CD-R disk, which can be written to until it is full and not recorded to again, and the CD-RW disk, which can be recorded and erased and re-recorded to many times. Both types of disk hold up to 700 MB per disc. Our center prefers the CD-R format and media over the CD-RW format and media for a couple of reasons:

■ It cannot be recorded over.

■ It is less expensive than CD-RW media.

When considering what type of optical drive to have for your center, it is a good idea to have a CD-RW drive on all of your machines, and at least one machine should have a DVD-R drive. DVD-R is a record-once format that can record up to 4.7 GB of information per disk, and so holds considerably more information than one CD-R/RW disk. The only drawback is that, unlike a CD-R to which you can record until it is filled, the DVD-R can only be written to once and not added to again. The DVD-R drive can read standard DVDs and can also be used as a CD-RW drive, too.

There are currently different DVD recording formats that you can choose from such as DVD-RAM, DVD+R, DVD+RW, DVD-RW, but they are not universally compatible with home DVD players or computer DVD-ROM drives, and only work on drives that support their respective format. However, DVD+R disks can be read by most DVD-based drives and support most DVD-based formats, but can only be recorded by a DVD drive that supports DVD+R. In conclusion, DVD-R or DVD+R are the best formats to choose because of their compatibility and capabilities, and are compatible with most home DVD players and computer DVD-ROM and DVD-R drives.

Computer hardware checklist

The following is a brief checklist that can aid you in selecting the right components for your computer:

- Pentium 4 class processor running at 2.0 GHz or higher;
- 512 MB minimum memory (1,024 MB recommended);
- 80 GB minimum hard drive;
- 18" or larger monitor;
- 128 MB video card;
- CD-RW and/or DVD-R optical drive.

Purchasing a scanner

The process of acquiring the right scanner can sometimes be a little more tedious than finding the right computer. Price is a major factor to consider when purchasing a scanner, too.

Types of scanner

There are several different types of scanner that you should be familiar with, so you can understand their differences and capabilities. The following provides a list of different scanner types used for digitization:

- flatbed scanner;
- overhead scanner;
- sheet-fed scanner;
- film scanner.

Flatbed scanner

A flatbed scanner is the most appropriate choice for use in digitization. They are widely used and versatile, and perform all the required tasks you need for digitization purposes. Flatbed scanners allow you to place single sheets or bound materials face down on the scan bed. Because you have the ability to scan bound materials effectively, flatbeds are the scanner of choice. In addition, flatbeds produce superb color and grayscale scans.

Overhead scanner

An overhead scanner that can produce the same color scans as a flatbed scanner is extremely expensive. A flatbed that can scan almost the same amount of area as an overhead scanner is much less expensive; however, if you are dealing with extremely fragile materials and do not want to damage them any further, an overhead scanner provides a great solution. If you purchase an overhead scanner for use and cannot afford a model that scans in color, make sure that it scans in grayscale. An overhead scanner that scans in line art or black and white only is not recommended for digitization purposes, especially for images. Overhead scanners are also large and bulky, and take up a great deal of space.

Sheet-fed scanner

A sheet-fed scanner is also not a good choice for digitization because you have to slide sheets of paper through the scanner, which makes it difficult to scan bound materials. Sheet-fed scanners also have the potential of damaging loose manuscripts, papers, and photographs, not to mention the excess handling involved that has the potential of damaging or ruining your materials.

Film scanner

Finally, film scanners are great for photographs, slides and negatives; however, film scanners are limited by size, and a 5 × 7 photograph is about as large as you can scan. You can use a flatbed scanner instead of a film scanner to scan archival and online quality images, and you can always purchase an adapter for your flatbed if you want to scan negatives and slides.

Pricing scanners

When discussing scanners, one of the most important aspects to consider before purchasing is the actual dimensions that the scanner is capable of scanning. This is usually referred to as the scan area. Most scan areas are determined by inches and/or media sizes such as

- 8½ × 11 (standard letter);
- 8½ × 14 (legal);
- 11 × 17 (ledger).

Most 8½ × 11 flatbed scanners are reasonably priced and can be purchased for less than a hundred dollars; however, their size is limited, and if you have documents that are larger than the scanner's bed, you have to make use of another scanner. An 8½ × 14 is more of an ideal size for regular scanning. Its larger scan area is better equipped to handle larger books and legal size documents. Most 8½ × 14 scanners can be purchased for a few hundred dollars. The ideal scanner is one that can handle 11 × 17 or larger. Its large scanning area permits you to scan more than one page at a time and can handle books that are larger and uniquely shaped better than a smaller scanner. Prices, however, climb into the thousands of dollars for this type of scanner.

A good alternative is to invest in one 11 × 17 scanner and one or more 8½ × 14 scanners. This way you can have at least one large-format scanner that you can use for bigger jobs and a couple of smaller scanners to use for smaller jobs. There are many 11 × 17 as well as 8½ × 14 scanners that are good choices for use in digitization, and a list of vendors and resource sites is located at the end of the chapter.

Scanner interface

The first thing to do when searching for the right scanner is to make absolutely sure that it is compatible with your current operating system, that its drivers work with your operating system, and that you are able to download driver updates from the vendor's website. Once you determine your need based on the information about your operating system, you need to decide which interface you want to use.

Digitization requires long hours using the scanner, so your scanner needs to be fast and reliable. Depending on the make and model of your scanner, it should have the ability to use the USB port and/or a SCSI connection, or, better yet, the IEEE 1394 FireWire port. You should avoid scanners for digitization that use the parallel port (printer port) or the older 1.1 USB port.

USB and parallel port scanners

Older scanners that use the parallel port and older 1.1 USB port are slow. You can lose valuable time waiting for the scanner just to complete one scanned image. Consequently, you lose time and money waiting on the scanner and paying your employees to scan. Always avoid implementing parallel port and 1.1 USB scanners for digitization purposes. However, the newer 2.0 USB ports are much faster and can handle the information more quickly. USB 2.0 is an acceptable solution if you decide to use the USB port; however, make sure that if you connect a scanner to the USB 2.0 port, it says Hi-Speed USB 2.0 for the scanner and USB port.

SCSI port scanner

SCSI scanners were the fastest and most widely used until a couple of years ago. Newer scanners and computers are phasing out the SCSI interface, which is a good reason not to invest in SCSI technology. However, if you currently have equipment that is SCSI based and can support the interface, you may want to use it as long as you can until you upgrade to newer equipment. SCSI is still fast and can perform well on older computers and operating systems, but the older it gets, the less it will be used and supported.

IEEE 1394 FireWire

FireWire is the newest and fastest technology available for scanning. It is comparable to the SCSI port for speed, and installation is easier to configure than most other interfaces. Newer scanners have the option of using this port. Most computers do not have or come with a FireWire card, so if you decide to go this route, be sure your computer comes with a FireWire card at the time of purchase, or you need to buy one and install it yourself. If you are lucky enough to purchase a scanner that includes a FireWire card, all you need to do is install it before you hook up your scanner. FireWire is a highly recommended choice we suggest you consider when deciding which scanner interface to use for your digitization center.

Scanner specifications

Have you ever wondered what bits and dpi mean when it comes to scanners?

If so, you are not alone. This information can sometimes be confusing and misleading. When looking at scanner specifications there are three important factors to consider:

- scan area;
- optical resolution (dots per inch);
- color depth (bits).

Scan area

We have already discussed scan area earlier in this chapter (8½ × 11, 8½ × 14 and 11 × 17). Remember, however, that the scan area is an important part of a scanner's specification.

Optical resolution (dots per inch)

When referring to optical resolution or dpi (dots per inch), you need to understand that this does not mean you achieve better color scans at a higher dpi (1,200 × 1,200) than a lower dpi (600 × 600). It should be noted: the higher the dpi the larger the image and file size. When scanning color images for your online digitization projects, you should scan at 300 dpi to keep images the same size as the original. You can always scan at 400 dpi or 600 dpi if you would like the image to be larger than the original. Black and white images are a different issue, so beginning with 400 dpi and going as high as 800 dpi is sufficient for online display.

Color depth (bits)

The majority of scanners have a color depth between 36-bit and 48-bit. This is somewhat misleading, and you need to know what this represents. When a scanner states it scans in 48-bit color, it is referring to the internal color depth that the scanner is capable of achieving. Most programs and video cards are only capable of displaying 24-bit color. This means you need to know how well your color scanner is able to scan and display 24-bit images. However, many 48-bit color scanners produce better quality scans than scanners that scan at a lower color depth. Look for reviews on a model you are considering to see its strengths and weaknesses, and to compare it to another potential scanner of your choice.

Scanner summary

When looking at scanners for digitization purposes, it is a good idea to find a scanner that has the following attributes:

- flatbed scanner;
- IEEE 1394 FireWire port or Hi-Speed USB 2.0 connection;
- an 8½ × 14 or 11 × 17 scan area;
- a 36-bit color depth or higher;
- a resolution of 600 × 1,200 dpi or higher.

Digital camera

Investing in a digital camera for your center can be a valuable asset and, not to mention, a good investment. Digital cameras provide several opportunities for you to enhance and promote your center. For example, using a digital camera is a good way for you to take all the pictures of your center, staff, etc., for use on your website, or for promotional purposes. You would not have to rely on finding images to use, and you could have total creative control over the photos posted on your center's website and other areas. However, the most important reason to invest in a digital camera for your center is for use on a project that has severely damaged materials, or for a project where the materials cannot be moved and you must perform the work where the materials are housed; it is for these two reasons that a digital camera could make a huge difference in your center.

When considering what type or model to purchase, there are a few things you should make sure the digital camera can do:

- Make sure there is support for RAW image file format and/or TIFF in addition to RAW.
- Make sure it has decent zoom lens capabilities.
- Make sure it has macro capabilities or is able to support a macro lens attachment for close-up shots.

TIFF and RAW image file formats

When looking at which image file formats a digital camera is capable of taking there is one image format that you should make sure your camera supports: the RAW image. Making sure your camera supports the RAW image format is a must because you can convert RAW images into archival TIFF images using your computer and certain software programs. The TIFF format is nice to have in addition to the RAW format because digital cameras can take 8-bit grayscale TIFF images. However, color TIFF capabilities on most digital cameras today only go as far as 16-bit color images. You need to have at least 24-bit color TIFF images for archival purposes. So, when looking for a digital camera, make sure that it supports the RAW image format, and if it has the ability to shoot TIFF images consider it a nice addition.

A digital camera that supports the TIFF image format can usually take 8-bit lossless compression grayscale images in the TIFF mode, and the RAW format provides you with a way to save RAW images as lossless TIFF images in color or black and white once you download them to your computer. If the camera does not take TIFF images but it does take RAW images then that is acceptable, but just make sure you can purchase Adobe® Photoshop® for saving your color TIFF images in at least 24-bit color. The RAW format is excellent because it is basically an unprocessed image, or it can be viewed as a digital negative. However, the RAW format is not universally accepted or a completely defined standard; the RAW format differs by manufacturer, i.e. Canon, Nikon, Minolta, Sony, etc., and even by camera make and model. However, this proprietary format is accompanied by software from your digital camera's manufacturer so you can process the image from your computer, and Adobe Photoshop CS includes support for working with RAW images.

RAW and TIFF images are large, so be prepared for a longer waiting period while the images are written to the camera's memory card. In addition, make sure you have a large memory card and possibly a few extra ones because these formats can take up a lot of room quickly. Depending on which setting you choose and whether it is color or black and white plays an important part in how large each photograph will be. You can count on the image file sizes to be around 5–20 MB per image. You can see how quickly your memory would get used up, and why the writing times to the memory card would be longer. A 512 MB or larger memory card for your digital camera should provide you with a good starting point, but depending on the project, location and computer access, you might want to invest in a card that is 1 GB or larger, or have multiple memory cards in different memory configurations.

Zoom lens

Your digital camera should have a zoom lens that is about the equivalent of a standard 35 mm film zoom lens, which means it can zoom to 140 mm or longer. This helps you zoom in on objects that are farther away when taking photographs.

Macro lens or macro mode

Having a macro mode or macro lens attachment available for your camera is extremely important because it allows you to take extremely close-up shots. This comes in very handy when taking archival images of pages that you need to OCR. Most digital cameras have the macro function built into the camera. Look for a flower icon on the camera or in the camera's menu function. If the camera does not support a macro function then a separate lens attachment is required. You need to make sure that the camera you choose can either support an additional macro lens or a macro lens attachment. In addition, mare sure there is a macro lens or macro attachment available for your camera.

Pricing

Digital cameras have come a long way since their inception. Prices have come down considerably and image quality has drastically improved. You should make it a point to research current models and invest in a high-quality digital camera for your center.

Alternative methods

In the event you cannot afford a digital camera or one that has the functions and capabilities you need, you can always use a film camera or make prints from a digital camera and scan them into the computer. This method is more time consuming, and could end up adding extra costs to a project, but it is another method that could be explored if needed.

Digital camera summary

When looking at a digital camera for digitization purposes, it is a good idea to find a camera that has the following attributes:

- supports RAW image file format;
- TIFF image format is nice to have in addition to RAW but not essential;
- macro lens or macro mode capabilities;
- third-party imaging software such as Adobe Photoshop;
- a digital zoom of the 35 mm film equivalent of 140 mm;
- a memory card of at least 512 MB or higher.

Other hardware considerations

Although the following components are not required to perform digitization tasks, you should take into consideration that disasters are possible and you need to protect your investment. In addition, you may also need to use a printer occasionally. The following list provides a few extra components that you should take into consideration when detailing a hardware list:

- surge protector or uninterruptible power supply (UPS) or battery backup;
- backup device (tape backup unit, CD-R, DVD-R);
- printer.

Surge protector/uninterruptible power supply

It is extremely important that each computer, scanner, and/or other device is connected to a surge protector. Surge protectors protect your equipment in the event of electrical surges, which could permanently damage your equipment and involve loss of data. A better alternative to a surge protector is an uninterruptible power supply (or battery backup) for your machines. Most battery backups include surge protection as well as keeping the machine powered on until you can safely shut it down. If you cannot afford to purchase uninterruptible power supplies for each machine, make sure you have at least one for the computer or server that stores all of your digitization files.

Backup device

Backing up your files is an absolutely necessary operation that you must perform routinely in order to have your files safely stored in case of disaster. In addition, it is a good idea to keep backed up files off-site in case of a fire or other disaster. You can use the CD-R and DVD-R media as a way to archive your files; this is a good way to back up your files intermittently and store off-site but not a good idea to use on a daily basis. You would spend far too much money on discs and have to manually sit at the computer to copy the information. A TBU (tape backup unit) is a better alternative. You can store large amounts of data on just one tape and purchase a few extra tapes and rotate them as needed. Plus, tapes can be used daily and last a long time before wearing out.

Printer

Printers are an indispensable tool and should have a place in your digitization center. The printer helps with editing and training purposes, and can be used when you find articles from websites and want to use them as a resource or reference. In addition, you will probably need to write letters occasionally, so having a printer for these purposes alone is worth it for your center. When deciding what type of printer to use in your digitization center, we recommend that you use a laser printer. Ink printers are too slow and the ink is expensive. Laser printers are much faster and cost less to maintain.

Summary and resources

- A computer is required for digitization.
- A scanner is required for digitization.

- A digital camera can be an extremely valuable tool in the digitization process.

- Know what components your computer needs to have to perform necessary digitization functions.

- Know what to look for when selecting the right scanner for your center.

- Know what other hardware components are beneficial for operating your center.

The following URLs provide excellent information on the hardware mentioned in this section, and on ordering and pricing equipment:

- Computers:
  - *http://www.cnet.com*
  - *http://www.dell.com*
  - *http://www.gateway.com*
  - *http://www.pcmag.com*
  - *http://www.pcworld.com*
  - *http://www.zdnet.com*
- Scanners:
  - *http://www.epson.com*
  - *http://www.hp.com*
  - *http://www.microtekusa.com*
  - *http://www.scanstore.com*
  - *http://www.scantips.com*
  - *http://www.umax.com*
  - *http://www.visioneer.com*

- Digital cameras:
  - *http://www.canon.com*
  - *http://www.dcresource.com*
  - *http://www.dcviews.com*
  - *http://www.dpreview.com*
  - *http://www.minolta.com*
  - *http://www.nikon.com*
  - *http://www.olympus.com*
  - *http://www.pentax.com*
  - *http://www.sony.com*

4

Software

Software is the key element in successfully creating documents for archiving and publishing online. The programs you choose not only determine how you create your publications, but also how you develop your training methods. The logistics of your center depend greatly on how you employ and execute your software programs, so pay close attention to the types of software available and which programs are best suited for your needs. Building your software library requires knowing what programs are available and how to price them. A good rule to follow when purchasing software is to find a product that performs well and offers less expensive upgrades when newer versions are available. Upgrading allows you to stay with a product that you like using, and over the long term, you save money because upgrades are less expensive than full versions. One of the biggest downfalls of software is that it is expensive, which can present a challenge when making your initial software purchases. Upgrading and staying with a particular product can save you time and valuable resources in the future, so look at the long term when shopping for and purchasing software.

Another alternative to consider when thinking about software is using freeware and/or shareware products in lieu of purchasing expensive programs. This approach, however, should only be used if the programs in question can adequately meet your needs.

Types of software required

The types of software programs you will need to create digital publications include:

- HTML editor;
- XML editor, parser and XSLT processor;
- text editor and/or word processor;
- image editor;
- scanning software;
- OCR software;
- FTP software;
- page layout and design software;
- PDF software.

HTML editor

An HTML (HyperText Markup Language) editor is any program that allows you to edit or write HTML code and documents. The two main types of HTML editors are text-based editors and WYSIWYG (What You See Is What You Get) editors. Text-based editors such as Microsoft Notepad, Microsoft Word and Corel® WordPerfect® allow you to only edit or write HTML code. You cannot actually see how the HTML document displays until you save the file and open it

in a browser such as Microsoft Internet Explorer, Netscape®
Navigator or Opera©. These text-based programs are used to
write HTML in its most basic format. There are other text-
based HTML editors that provide more advanced features
and were specifically designed for writing HTML. These
editors make use of tags and features that allow the user to
click a button for tags, bold, italics, and so forth, instead of
always typing each tag or command by hand. This is helpful
and allows you to avoid repetition and reduces the amount
of errors that occur when typing by hand. A couple of these
programs are NoteTab Pro® and Arachnophilia©. Free
versions of both are available online. These editors have one
big advantage over word processing programs used as
HTML editors: they produce clean HTML code. Only the
HTML you type into them will appear in your documents.
Word processing programs may insert code you did not type,
which can cause unintended results when the file is opened
in a browser.

WYSIWYG programs allow you to actually look at the
HTML document as you edit it and make changes that you
can directly see onscreen. Examples of WYSIWYG
programs include: Microsoft FrontPage®, Netscape
Composer and Macromedia® Dreamweaver®. WYSIWYG
programs have some advantages over text-based editors,
such as an easier learning curve and being able to see your
work as you are creating; however, their functions
sometimes do not display correctly on other browsers that
are not native to the program with which they are affiliated.
For example, a web page created with Microsoft FrontPage
might not display some features correctly in Netscape

Navigator (see Figures 4.1 and 4.2). This would cause the page to display undesired results that would not represent what the designer had in mind. In addition, these programs sometimes use browser-specific code that is unnecessary and difficult to understand or change if you decide you want to edit the code by hand at a later date.

Figure 4.1 An image created in FrontPage using the drawing tools displayed incorrectly in Netscape Navigator

Figure 5: First tab selected

at the top of the NoteTab Pro window, c

id Window option *(see Figure 6)*. This
creen and the text file on the right screen

You achieve the best results when you create the HTML from scratch. Not only does it give you total control over what goes into your HTML document, but it also provides you with valuable skills that are helpful when writing, editing, or finding problems in several lines of code. You have a better sense of what makes HTML work and how to create pages that are dynamic and visually appealing.

Figure 4.2 The same image as seen in Figure 4.1 displayed correctly in Internet Explorer

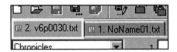

Figure 5: First tab selected

ıt the top of the NoteTab Pro window, ɩ

d Window option *(see Figure 6)*. This reen and the text file on the right scree

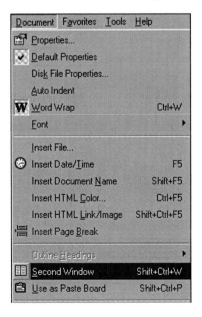

XML software

An XML editor works much like an HTML editor, and some programs can be used for both authoring purposes. Some popular XML editors, such as XMetaL® (*http://www .softquad.com*) or XML Spy® (*http://www.xmlspy.com/*), will assist you through the markup process, and show tags in a graphical and hierarchical display. These editors cost several hundred dollars, and usually include parsing software that validates your markup against the DTD you have specified. The online Buyer's Guide on the XML.com website at *http://www.xml.com/buyersguide/* has reviews of a number of XML editors. Some word processing programs claim to offer XML authoring but are not really well suited to that purpose. Often they will add extraneous code that you do not want cluttering up your documents.

If you have no money for software, you can write XML documents in a plain text editor. NoteTab offers a free version of their software from their website *http://www.notetab.com*. For a minimal cost you can upgrade to NoteTab Pro, which shows XML tags in a contrasting color to regular text and allows you to program frequently used commands. The excellent Help files include instructions in writing these commands, called Clips, to automatically enter tags, entities, or special character codes, and even to launch other programs such as your parser. You can also set up templates, something we often do for digital projects. While it does involve more effort than the out-of-the-box editors, it also offers some amenities at very little cost.

In addition to an editor, you will need a parser to check that your XML is valid, and an XSLT processor to transform your XML to HTML. Robin Cover's XML Cover Pages (*http://www.oasis-open.org/cover/xml.html*) describe a number of parsers and provide links to their websites. Many of these are free. As previously noted, most of the commercial XML editors will have a parsing function built in. The XML Cover Pages – an excellent resource for all things XML – also discuss conversion tools for transforming XML using XSLT. One of the most popular tools is Saxon, a program developed by Michael Kay, author of *The XSLT Programmer's Reference*, and available for free from his website (*http://saxon.sourceforge.net/*).

Text editor and/or word processor

Text-editing programs are sometimes referred to as word processors. These programs allow you to create, format, and edit text. As mentioned earlier, you can use any word processing program to write HTML. The text-editing program works with the OCR software to create text files. A word processor is what you need to save and edit the text that you will use for marking up your XML and HTML documents. Microsoft Notepad is a basic text editor that comes with the Windows operating system; however, it has limited capabilities. Microsoft Word and Corel WordPerfect offer more robust formatting features and provide enhanced text-editing tools such as spell-checking.

Image editor

Image editing programs are among the most valuable programs you can have when producing and editing images for archiving and publishing online. Image editors allow you to perform many tasks such as saving in multiple file formats, resizing images, enhancing photographs, cropping, creating images for your website, and so on. This is one tool that you cannot be without when starting and running a digitization center. When looking for an image editor there are a few things to keep in mind. Most imaging programs are expensive. Adobe Photoshop is fairly expensive; however, once you purchase a licence, upgrades are less expensive than the retail version.

Because Adobe Photoshop is such a powerful design tool, it requires long hours to learn its many features and capabilities. Jasc® PaintShop™ Pro® is an excellent program that performs many of the functions found in Photoshop, but PaintShop is a much easier program to use and learn than Photoshop, and is much less expensive. PaintShop Pro retails for considerably less than Photoshop. A good solution is to purchase one licence for Photoshop and use it when you need its capabilities and purchase PaintShop Pro for your other machines.

Scanning software

In order to ensure the proper operation of your scanner, you must be sure to install the software and drivers that are included with your scanner; the drivers and software work together to provide seamless and optimal operation of your scanner. However, most software that accompanies scanners is limited in its capabilities and functions, or is a trimmed-down version of a more powerful program, and therefore additional third-party software is needed.

Because certain file formats are required for archival purposes, you must have a program that supports and recognizes the specific formats required for digitization purposes. When looking for programs to supplement your scanner, make sure it is compatible with your operating system and TWAIN scanner.

WOCAR© 2.5 is a freeware program that scans images in the CCITT Group 4 TIFF compression scheme. WOCAR automatically defaults to this format, so you never need to change any file settings – just scan your documents directly into WOCAR to get your archival TIFF images. WOCAR also doubles as an OCR program, and will be discussed as one in the next section.

WOCAR is a good program to use, but it is limited in its functionality and use, so you should also consider other options if your resources allow. One alternative is to use a scanning suite that saves in several different file formats other than TIFF, and performs a variety of different functions. ScanSoft® PaperPort® is an excellent scanning suite that combines many useful functions for use in scanning.

OCR software

The OCR program is what you will use when you convert your archived images into text with your word processor. The OCR program takes the text from the archival image and converts it to text in your word processor. When it comes to OCR software, you will want to make sure you buy a program with a great reputation and proven track record. The better the OCR program, the more time and money you will save. In addition, a good OCR program makes fewer mistakes and allows you to save time when editing your text files. Two widely used and highly recognized OCR software programs are OmniPage Pro® and Prime Recognition®. If you are on an extremely limited budget, you can use WOCAR as your OCR program; however, it is not as accurate and robust as OmniPage Pro or Prime Recognition. WOCAR is a freeware program and is available for download from the TUCOWS website at the following URL: *http://tucows.wave.net.br/system/preview/234813.html*.

FTP software

An FTP or File Transfer Protocol program is what you will use when you are ready to upload your files and projects to the Internet for viewing. The FTP client connects to your server and allows you to create directories and move your files into the appropriate folder where they can be viewed on the Internet. There are several free versions of FTP software available for academic institutions, students, teachers, and government and non-profit organizations. WS_FTP® LE is an excellent free FTP program. You can download it from the following URL: *http://www.ftpplanet.com/download.htm*.

Page layout and design software

Page layout programs are useful for when you want to create publications in-house and/or you need to digitize publications that are in a page layout format. You can also use these tools to publicize your site. Page layout programs offer more design features than word processors. In addition, page layout programs are helpful if you want to create brochures, leaflets, business cards, etc. When using page layout programs you have the ability to make publications for your center in-house, and you will not have to pay to outsource designing for your publication material. A few page layout programs that are available for use are

- Adobe PageMaker®
- Adobe InDesign®
- QuarkXPress™.

PDF software

PDF, or Portable Document Format, is a widely-used format that allows people to exchange information in instances where the other person might not have the proper program to open the file, or when a person does not want others to be able to modify and change their files. For digitization purposes, the PDF provides a quick and easy solution for getting files online for viewing and downloading. The PDF is not a replacement for an HTML or XML document and should be used as a companion with current formats to enhance site accessibility. Adobe Acrobat® is the leading software program for creating a PDF. Acrobat provides many options when creating PDFs, and it works with Microsoft Office applications to create a PDF with just the click of a button. The attractive aspect of PDF files is that anyone with a computer can view them by downloading the free Adobe Reader® from Adobe at the following URL: *http://www.adobe.com/products/acrobat/readstep2.html*.

Purchasing software

Purchasing software is a relatively simple task. Locate retailers that offer the software you need, and check their prices against other retailers. Most online retailers are competitive and often run specials, so be on the lookout when you begin pricing software, and watch current trends, too, because a newer version may be coming out soon, and it would be a good idea to know release dates for new versions. It is also a good idea to check the vendors' websites for possible upgrades or newer versions that could be coming out soon. You want to use the latest software versions available, and once you purchase a program, you benefit from free updates and support, and you are eligible for great discounts on upgrades to the latest version without having to find the full price each time you want to buy a new program for your center.

When purchasing software for your center, be sure it is compatible with your operating system, and that your computers have the minimum requirements to run the software. All you have to do is look on the box to see what platforms it is compatible with and what the minimum processor and memory requirements are. You can look at the vendor's website for more detailed information about the product in general. You can also look at online stores to see what the minimum requirements are to operate the software.

Summary and resources

- Software is one of the most important aspects of a digitization center.

- Knowing what programs are available and which ones perform well can greatly affect the outcome of your projects.

- Keeping price and upgrading information in mind should make your software decisions easier.

The following list provides a reference to some of the software applications available for use in creating your digital publications and where you can locate them online:

- HTML editing programs:

  - Arachnophilia: *http://www.arachnoid.com*

  - Macromedia Dreamweaver: *http://www.macromedia .com/software/dreamweaver*

  - Microsoft FrontPage: *http://www.microsoft.com/ frontpage*

  - Netscape Composer: *http://wp.netscape.com/browsers/ using/newusers/composer*

  - NoteTab Pro: *http://www.notetab.com*

- Imaging programs:

  - Adobe Photoshop: *http://www.adobe.com/products/ photoshop*

  - Jasc Paint Shop Pro: *http://www.jasc.com*

- Page layout programs:
  - Adobe InDesign: *http://www.adobe.com/products/indesign*
  - Adobe PageMaker: *http://www.adobe.com/products/pagemaker*
  - QuarkXPress: *http://www.quark.com*
- PDF programs:
  - Adobe Acrobat: *http://www.adobe.com/products/acrobat*
- Text editing/word processing programs:
  - Corel WordPerfect: *http://www.corel.com*
  - Microsoft Notepad: *http://www.microsoft.com*
  - Microsoft Word: *http://www.microsoft.com/office/word*
- OCR programs:
  - OmniPage Pro: *http://www.scansoft.com*
  - Prime Recognition: *http://www.primerecognition.com/*
- Scanning suites:
  - ScanSoft PaperPort: *http://www.scansoft.com*
  - WOCAR 2.5 is available as a free download at the following URL: *http://tucows.wave.net.br/system/preview/234813.html*
- XML editing programs:
  - NoteTab Pro: *http://www.notetab.com*
  - XmetaL: *http://www.softquad.com*
  - XML Spy: *http://www.xmlspy.com*

- XSLT processors:
  - Saxon: *http://saxon.sourceforge.net/*
- FTP programs:
  - WS_FTP: *http://www.ipswitch.com*
- Freeware and shareware programs:
  - *http://www.download.com*
  - *http://www.tucows.com*

5

The digitization process

Flowchart of the digitization process

Digitization is a long and complicated process. There are many steps involved, as illustrated in the flowchart shown in Figure 5.1. Every project is different, but the four basic stages include the following:

- *Stage 1* – select material.
- *Stage 2* – convert normal text into electronic text.
- *Stage 3* – format electronic text for the Internet.
- *Stage 4* – create website for access and navigation.

To learn more about the steps involved in each stage of the process, look at each box in the flowchart. A detailed description of each of the steps is given in the sections which follow.

Selection of materials

In order to be considered for digitization, materials must go through a selection process. When selecting materials for your center it is a good idea to understand that the material has to meet certain requirements. To determine eligibility for the OSU Library, materials should fulfill the following criteria:

■ It should meet the research needs of faculty, students, and scholars within and beyond the OSU community. In

Figure 5.1 EPC digitization flowchart

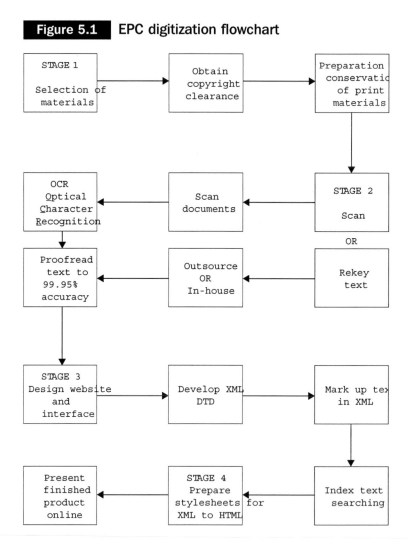

assessing what material meets the needs of our constituency, consideration should be given to the scholarly content of the material, the uniqueness of the material, and the demand for the material.

- It should benefit from increased access and should contribute to the OSU Library's service and collection development missions. Materials that are difficult to access in their original formats or that would benefit from increased speed or depth of access via electronic delivery formats should be given priority.

- It should have clear ownership and copyright clearance. Before undertaking a digitization project, the Library needs to secure sound legal advice about the ownership and rights to reproduce or publish materials electronically.

- It should be of interest to potential partners. Materials that would be of interest to campus and outside partners, both collaborators on the content and potential sources of funding and other support, should be given strong consideration.

In addition, before selecting materials, consideration for their preservation is made from the following perspectives: (a) items should not be digitized whereby the scanning process is detrimental to the item itself; (b) items that receive heavy patron use and are quickly deteriorating should be selected for imaging in order to preserve the original. Although data migration is an ongoing concern, original editions will not be considered reformatted to preservation quality levels by digitization until the technological issues have been resolved and appropriate standards are widely accepted.

A specific checklist of attributes, access, infrastructure, and preservation concerns are included in the 'Suggested Collections/Materials to be Digitized' form, available on the OSU Library's website at *http://digital.library.okstate.edu/ suggest.html*. The Collection Development Committee makes decisions as to which suggested materials will be chosen for digitization. In addition, the committee employs established collection development criteria and policies. Selection for digitization requires that materials have enduring value and be available in a sufficient number or quantity that they form a significant and unique research corpus. Moreover, the decision to digitize takes into account many factors, as evidenced by the criteria on the 'Suggested Collections/Materials to be Digitized' form.

In selecting materials, the OSU Library actively seeks out partners, both collaborators on specific projects and supporting partners to supply funding or technical assistance. Institutions such as the Oklahoma Department of Libraries, the State Historical Society, other academic libraries, and other organizations in Oklahoma or out of state are approached for long-range planning on digitization projects. Foundations and/or corporate sponsors are also approached, and the Director of Library Development and Outreach will facilitate the Library's efforts to prepare grants and solicit monies from funding agencies and corporations. In addition, the Library respects the cultural traditions of different ethnic and racial groups in preparing its digital collections; consultation with tribal or other interested organizations will be conducted prior to digitizing potentially sensitive materials.

Preservation/conservation of originals

Great care and consideration must be taken when preparing original materials for digitization. In addition, you must exercise extreme caution when performing the actual digitization of the materials. When materials undergo digitization, the process could damage the originals; you do not, under any circumstances, want to further damage rare materials. Digitization is a process of retaining the key attributes of the original material, and digitization should in no way be seen as a replacement of printed materials. The main goal of digitization is to provide greater access to materials that are rare and act as a supplement to the original.

Standards

Standards allow for the dissemination of knowledge through formats that conform to specific guidelines for usage. Standards also provide us with the option of how we would like to have our materials displayed online and what formats are available for us to choose. Tables 5.1 to 5.3 represent available formats and guidelines that you can choose from when planning your projects for archiving and online viewing.

Information architecture

After you have completed housing your center and setting up the framework of your computer systems, it is time to work on the actual structure of your center's projects.

Table 5.1 Image formats

File name and extension	Extended name	Description
TIFF .tif and .tiff	Tagged Image File Format	The CCITT Group 4 compression scheme is the standard of choice for black and white archival images of text – the TIFF is also used for archiving color images using a 24-bit color depth in a LZW compression scheme, or completely uncompressed
JPEG .jpg and .jpeg	Joint Photographic Experts Group	The JPEG should only be used for online and/or viewing purposes – it is also the most widely used and accepted image file on the Internet
GIF .gif	Graphics Interchange Format	GIF files should only be used for online and/or viewing purposes – limited to 256 colors

Figure 5.2 Text formats

File name and extension	Extended name	Description
Text .txt	Plain Text	The plain text file is the format of choice for storing text-based documents using the ASCII standard
RTF .rtf	Rich Text Format	A text file that has formatting features much like Word and WordPerfect, but is not as robust as Word or WordPerfect

Figure 5.2 Text formats (*continued*)

File name and extension	Extended name	Description
Word Document .doc	Microsoft Word Document	Word allows the user to create and edit text more effectively and efficiently than a simple text editor – useful for creating and editing plain text documents
WordPerfect Document .wpd	Corel WordPerfect Document	WordPerfect allows the user to create and edit text more effectively and efficiently than a simple text editor – useful for creating and editing plain text documents

Table 5.3 Markup formats

File name and extension	Extended name	Description
HTML .htm and .html	Hypertext Markup Language	Uses codes and tags to make web pages, which is how the Internet is able to function and communicate
XML .xml	Extensible Markup Language	Uses codes and tags to create and archive electronic publications – also used in electronic commerce
SGML .sgm and .sgml	Standard Generalized Markup Language	The first markup language – it uses tags to identify a document's structure

Because your projects will be viewed online, you must develop a cohesive manner in which your site is to be displayed. Before any of the physical work begins on your projects, you must first define how you are going to set up the file structure of each project. Your projects need to reside on a file server that your staff can access on a daily basis and exchange files and information with. Once you have a file server in place, you need to create a folder or folders on your server that specifically pertain to each project and/or work-related material. If you have one or more projects lined up, you need to create separate root directory folders for each project, and only store information directly related to the project inside the folder. For example, our entire Kappler project resides on our file server inside the KAPPLER folder. Inside the KAPPLER folder contains all the information on the project. For this project, we set up a directory structure that is intuitive and easy to navigate.

Important note: The way you set up your directory structure for your HTML files for each project is exactly how it will be navigated when it is online.

From the earliest point in a project's life, it is extremely important that you plan carefully when setting up a directory structure. Navigation is critical to a project's success, and spending quality time at this point is a necessity. In addition, when you do things right the first time, you will not have to go back later and correct each document, which takes time and resources, and could cause errors or problems if not thoroughly checked.

To begin, you need to outline exactly what goes into a project, and everything about each particular project goes into the one folder you created to house that project. So, the first thing you need to do is create your root directory or main folder that contains all the information on the project. Once you have created the root directory, it is time to create subfolders within the root directory. At this point, all you need to do is click or double click the root directory folder and create new folders within that folder. Repeat the above steps each time you want to create a new folder or subfolder.

When beginning a project that involves scanning a book or multiple documents, you need to create four separate subfolders in that project's root directory folder. If your project has multiple volumes or additions, you can create a subfolder for each volume, and then place the four basic folders in each volume's folder, or you can create the four basic folders in the root directory and place each volume's folder within that folder. The four folders you need to create are as follows:

- image_files
- text_files
- xml_files
- html_files

Important note: The use of an underscore (_) is important for accessibility and to avoid having an empty space in a file name. You should use an underscore any time you need to connect words when naming a file. For example, if you want to name a file or folder 'to do list', you should use underscores where the words break: to_do_list.

These four folders contain all the information about the project. The image_files folder contains all the archival TIFF images that are created when scanning the original documents. The text_files folder contains all the text files that are OCR'd and proofed against the original documents. The xml_files folder contains all the XML files that are marked up from the text files, and finally the html_files folder contains all the HTML documents that are converted from the XML files for online viewing. This structure identifies file types, and helps you and your staff locate particular files and keeps them separate from files with other extensions. So, text files would only go in the text_files folder, and so on. There might be times when you need to keep other types of files associated with a certain project inside the project's folder. That is fine as long as you put them in the root directory or create a separate folder in the root directory to keep them separate from the actual project files. Naming files and folders is another important area of information architecture. (Refer to the section on naming and saving files later in this chapter for more detailed information about file naming conventions and upper and lower case extensions.)

Scanning/rekeying

Scanning is the first step toward putting a document into an electronic format. Through scanning we are able to take the printed document and digitize its contents so we can work with the text and images to prepare the document for presentation and publication on the Internet.

Be aware that we use the term image to refer to two different items. The first is the product of a scanned document. For instance, the item you place on the scanner is the printed document, but the picture you produce on screen once you have scanned the document is the image.

The second item we call an image is almost anything within a document that is not text; this term includes photographs, drawings, pictures, maps, graphs, charts, and so forth.

To scan or rekey?

The condition of the materials ultimately determines how they are to be converted into electronic format. Extremely fragile materials, anything printed before 1940 (some material before 1940 is capable of being scanned, but it cannot be handwritten and must be in good condition), and any manuscripts probably will have to be retyped, because the optical character recognition (OCR) software used to convert a scanned image to text is sometimes unable to recognize the textual characters. Overhead scanning devices are less damaging to books than flatbed scanners. In extreme cases of fragility, or if extremely frail materials cannot be moved to your center for obvious reasons, a digital camera is another means of getting material into electronic format.

If the print is clear enough to OCR, the documents are scanned, OCR'd, then saved as text files. Whether scanned and OCR'd or rekeyed, all text is proofread. Our goal at the Oklahoma State University Library Electronic Publishing Center is *99.95 percent* accuracy. This usually requires that the material is proofread three times by at least two different people.

Scanning

Once you have your digitization center's infrastructure in place and a project lined up, you are ready to take the first step in creating your online publications. Scanning is the process of transferring your printed materials into electronic format. Scanning is usually a long, slow process that can take weeks or even months to complete depending on the size of your project. A large scanner can cut down the amount of time needed for scanning material into the computer. Scanning pages of text is repetitive and mundane; the less time it takes to scan your material, the better.

There are differences in scanning text for archiving and scanning images for display. When scanning material for archival purposes there are a few things you need to know. It is best to scan text at 400 dpi, in black and white document (not photo) settings, and to save the image in the TIFF format using the compression scheme CCITT Group 4. The CCITT Group 4 TIFF format is best suited for archiving because it keeps the image file sizes small. Other formats and compression schemes create large file sizes, and this would mean you could save less in your storage space. Also, large files take time to open and are less stable when larger than a few megabytes. In addition, large image file sizes corrupt easily and could cause you to lose valuable information by not allowing you to open the files you created or causing your operating system to crash. Thus try to keep your archived images as small as your archival format allows; however, this does not imply that you should scan at the minimum requirement allowed by your format – you should always scan at what is recommend for archiving in your chosen format.

Scanning images for display differs from scanning for archival purposes. When scanning black and white or color photos, make sure you adjust your setting to scan for photographs. There are also adjustments between black and white and color photos; choose the appropriate setting for the type of photograph you are scanning. Black and white photos can usually be scanned at 300 dpi or 400 dpi, and up to 800 dpi depending on how large you want the image to be. Black and white photos and text documents should always be scanned in 8-bit grayscale. Color photos should be scanned at 300 dpi or 400 dpi. When scanning color photos for archival purposes make sure that your scanner scans in at least 24-bit color and you save the image in TIFF format. All black and white and color TIFF images for archiving should always be saved using a lossless compression scheme such as LZW or Packbits. CCITT Group 3, CCITT Group 4 and Modified Huffman, which are fax compressions, are also lossless compressions schemes, but are only used for saving black and white text documents.

If the image was satisfactorily scanned, all you have to do now is rename the file using the file naming standard you created and save the file to the server or drive that is housing your project. Be sure to save the file in its designated folder inside its project's folder.

Rekeying

Sometimes the materials you want to digitize might not be in good repair, contain handwritten notes or additions, or be completely handwritten. Handwriting does not OCR well, and needs to be rekeyed by hand. Rekeying is the process of taking a document and physically typing the information contained in the document directly into your word processor. Rekeying is extremely involved and time consuming. If a document or documents from a project need to be rekeyed, then you need to allot extra time for the rekeying of the text and proofreading. When rekeying text, you should open your word processing program and begin typing the text *exactly* as it appears on the document. Be sure to preserve the structure and content as closely as possible to the original. Do not get in a hurry or feel rushed when rekeying text; take the necessary time to make sure you do it right as you go. Always use the spell-checker in your word processor to help ensure fewer mistakes; however, it is not a good idea to rely solely on the spell-checker to catch spelling errors because it will not catch all misspelled words or certain variants of words. For example, some commonly overlooked words might include: form and from, you and your, and site and sight. These are just a few examples of why it is important to proofread the text in addition to using the spell-checker. Rekeying is a long, slow process and should only be performed when absolutely necessary. If you need to rekey text, consider outsourcing the work; there are a number of companies that provide this service. Most companies send the materials to another country such as India to be rekeyed. They find that typists make fewer mistakes when they do not speak the language they are rekeying. You can always count on rekeying handwritten material, but the use of a digital camera might provide a solution or alternative to rekeying older or damaged printed materials.

Conclusion

In conclusion, scanning is the act of taking print materials and transferring them into an electronic format. Materials for scanning should be in good condition and not handwritten. Rekeying is physically typing the contents of the printed materials into a word processor. Rekeying is necessary when the printed materials are old, in poor condition or are handwritten.

Imaging

To make an image that is easily viewable and retains as much of its original qualities as possible for display on the Internet, we usually use Jasc Paint Shop Pro or Adobe Photoshop to resize, crop, and/or edit before making the image available online. This way we can preserve the integrity and clarity of the picture for online viewing.

Imaging can be one of the most complicated areas in digitization, but it is also one of the most rewarding. Presenting nice, clear images online enhances the visual appeal of your site, and creates interest in the way you present your photographs to your online viewing audience. There are basically two main areas of imaging for digitization centers:

- archival imaging;
- presentation imaging.

Archival imaging

Archival imaging consists of scanning your documents and photographs into their respective archival image format. The OSU Library Electronic Publishing Center uses the TIFF format for our archival image format. We use the CCITT Group 4 compression scheme for text-based images and a lossless TIFF compression scheme such as LZW for photographic images. Black and white TIFF text-based images and photographic images should be scanned in 8-bit grayscale. Color TIFF images should be scanned in 24-bit color. Again, any time you scan for archival purposes, be sure to scan using a lossless compression mode. Scanning TIFF images completely uncompressed is another way to save images for archival purposes, but be forewarned that uncompressed TIFF images are extremely large. It is not uncommon for one 24-bit color uncompressed TIFF image to be around 40–100 MB or larger, especially if you scan at 400 dpi or higher. Uncompressed TIFF images are huge and you need the latest and greatest computer loaded with tons of memory to work effectively and efficiently with uncompressed TIFF images.

This process is relatively simple: you use your scanner to scan the documents into the TIFF format through the scanning program that allows you to save into the Group 4 TIFF format. WOCAR and ScanSoft's PaperPort are two programs that allow you to scan into CCITT Group 4 TIFF format. Once you have named and saved your image, you can use an imaging program to make any necessary adjustments. One of the most frequently performed tasks is straightening your images. When you scan bound material it is often difficult to get it as straight as you want it to be. This is where the magic of imaging comes to the rescue.

Just about every imaging program on the market has the functions necessary to straighten or align crooked images. This is important for several reasons. First, if you ever decide you want to make the actual page images available for your patrons to view, you will definitely want to make sure each and every image is as straight as it can possibly be. Second, when archiving information that is going to be around for future generations to see and possibly work with, it is important that the work you perform be to the absolute best of your abilities. You do not want to leave behind a legacy that shows haphazard care or concern. Taking your time at the beginning makes all the difference, and it saves you countless hours of labor and frustration if you have to go back and fix and/or repair any problems, not to mention the fact that you might not have the original materials around to make the corrections you need or want to make after the project has been completed.

Once you have scanned your images for archival purposes, you are ready to enhance or make any necessary changes to the images with a photo editing program. You can take your images and straighten them if need be, or create your derivative JPEG images for web display. Or, if you prefer, you can rescan just the photo, chart or other images within the text and save them into the JPEG format after you scan and resize the image to the size you want to have displayed online. Photo editing allows you to adjust and get just the right look or format for your center.

Presentation imaging

This step generally involves taking the archival TIFF image and using an image software program such as PaintShop Pro or Photoshop to edit, resize, and save as a JPEG for online display. In some cases, you might want to rescan the images for display-only purposes. Sometimes it is easier to just scan an image rather than to edit it with software. In some cases you can use a digital camera for presenting your images online. Whichever method you choose, there are a few basic steps you should know that can assist you in creating nicely detailed images for online presentation.

Straightening images

Sometimes it can seem as though an image will not come out as straight as you would like for it to be no matter how many times you scan it. This can be frustrating, but there is a way for you to get rid of crooked images once and for all. Using an image editing program such as PaintShop Pro or Photoshop allows you to straighten the image to your liking. When using your image editing program look for a *Rotate* or *Straighten Image* function. The *Rotate* function allows you to specify exactly how much or little you want to rotate the image. Simply indicate the direction and how many degrees you would like to rotate the image, and the image rotates to its new position. If it does not come out as straight as you like, keep rotating it until you get it as straight as you want. The *Straighten Image* function straightens the image automatically; if you like the result you can save the image and use it, or, if you do not like the result, you should rotate it manually using the *Rotate* function. Rotating an image should be the first step when editing an image.

Important note: Do not resize or perform any other functions to the image before straightening or rotating as the image could suffer from a loss of quality or produce undesired results.

Resizing images

When an image is too large, resizing can help you attain the right picture size for your imaging purposes. TIFF images are much better suited for resizing than JPEG images. The TIFF image contains much more information than a JPEG, and the TIFF can be manipulated in several different ways while still maintaining great image quality. The JPEG is not easily manipulated in some instances, and it is better to work with a TIFF when creating images for online display. It is also important to note that when you are finished editing a TIFF for online viewing, you will save it in JPEG format. Thus you are able to keep your original TIFF file, make the necessary changes to the image using your imaging software, and then save the image as a JPEG. Be careful not to save over your TIFF as you are editing it because you do not want to make any changes to your archival image. It is a good idea to copy the images you are editing into a separate folder, so you do not have to worry about accidentally saving over your archival image. If you are starting from scratch, scan your images in as TIFF files, and then begin editing them.

Resizing images is a fairly simple process. Open the TIFF file in your image editing program and select the *Resize* function. There are a few ways you can go about resizing your image. The easiest way to resize your image is by percentage. For example, if your image is twice as large as you want, you can choose to reduce it by 50 percent to get it to the required size. Sometimes it takes some tinkering with the percentage sizes to get the size you want. You can always resize, then resize again. Or, you can choose lower or higher percentages until you find one that resizes your images best. You can always undo any resizing by clicking the back arrow button from the toolbar. This helps you avoid closing and reopening images.

You can also resize by pixel size if you are more accustomed to using pixel sizes or know the exact pixel size you would like to display your images. Simply enter the pixel size for the image and click *OK*.

Another way you can resize an image is by the actual or print size of an image. This method allows you to reproduce the image at the exact size that it appears in the original printed material or photograph. You can normally choose from inches or centimeters. All you need to do is enter the width and height of the original and click *OK*.

Cropping images

Cropping an image allows you to take out any unnecessary space on the image, and gives you the option of displaying only what is needed. Another nice feature about cropping is that it also reduces the file size of an image when you are trimming unnecessary space that is not needed for viewing purposes. When cropping an image, click the cropping tool and select the area you want to keep. Double click the image and the image is cropped. That is all there is to it – cropping is one of the easiest tasks you can perform in imaging.

Saving images

When you are finished resizing and cropping your image, and finished making any additional changes, you are ready to save your image. All you need to do here is name it according to the naming structure you set up for displaying images online, locate the folder in which images for display for this particular project reside, and save it in the JPEG format.

Conversion to electronic text

To convert a document image to electronic text we use Optical Character Recognition (OCR) software to bring up the TIFF image of the scanned document, select the necessary text portion, and put it into a format where we can edit the text for accuracy and usability.

We use a technique called zoning to select the text then save it as a plain text (.txt) document to edit in a word processor such as Microsoft Word, Corel WordPerfect, Notepad, or WordPad. Zoning is the act of selecting an area or areas of text on an image that you want OCR'd.

OCR is the act of taking your archival TIFF images and converting them into readable and editable text. In the process of OCR'ing, you are not changing or altering your image files; instead, you are using a program to read the text in an image and create text files that are used for long-term storage and to mark up your documents for online viewing. OCR'ing an image is a fairly simple process. For example, you open your OCR program and select the image you want OCR'd. Next, you zone the areas of text. Finally, you save the file as a .txt file and begin editing and proofreading your file.

Those are the basic steps involved in OCR'ing an image. Of course, there are some steps such as naming your file and deciding which folder to save it to that you should have already outlined in your project's initial setup. These issues are further discussed in the sections on naming and saving files and information architecture, respectively. It should be noted that you can usually select more than one image to OCR at a time, but be careful not to do too many images at once. OCR'ing several images at a time could cause your computer to crash, and that is when you could lose some information. You can safely OCR about ten pages at a time. If an article is more than ten pages in length, continue to create new text files until you are finished OCR'ing the entire article. Once you have finished OCR'ing, you can combine the text files into one text file by copying and pasting the information from the other text files in the order you OCR'd the article.

Proofreading

Once you have OCR'd a document, you need to proofread it, or proof for short. When you proof a document, you check each letter, number, word, punctuation mark, symbol and so forth to be sure it matches exactly with the corresponding character in the printed document.

Proofing a document requires concentration and patience to check each and every paragraph, sentence, word, and punctuation mark to ensure they exactly match their counterpart in the printed document. We strive for *99.95 percent* accuracy with the printed document, so you should proof each document very carefully *both* during OCR'ing and during mark-up.

The best way to proof a document that is electronic is to have the original directly in front of you or on a bookstand. The book or document should be in close enough proximity that you can easily read the text and compare it to the text on the screen. After you have opened the text file or files that you are proofing, increase the font size of the text to 12 point or larger. This allows for the letters, numbers and characters to display larger onscreen so your eyes are not strained as much as if you were looking at smaller type.

Note: The next step is only available if you use a high-end word processor such as Microsoft Word or Corel WordPerfect. Notepad and WordPad do not have the following capability.

If you do not want to adjust the point size of the font, you can always increase the percentage size of the document as it is displayed. This way prevents you from having to globally change the font size of the document. The following steps can increase the viewing area of your document in Word. From the menu bar, select *View*, then *Zoom*. The *Zoom* dialog box opens and allows you to increase or decrease the viewing area of the document

Another way to use this function without using the menu is to look at the toolbar and find the drop-down menu that has a number with a percent sign. You can pull down the menu and select a larger or smaller percentage to adjust the viewing screen. Or, you can click once inside the pull-down menu and enter a custom percentage to adjust the viewing area. If the toolbar is not displayed, you can click *View* from the menu bar, go to *Toolbars*, and make sure the *Standard* option is checked.

Proofreading is perhaps the most mission-critical step of the entire digitization process. It is of the utmost importance that the online version of the text maintains and fully represents the original document. We cannot stress enough how important this step is to the quality of a project. Many people, such as scholars, students, and historians, will cite, refer interested parties to, and use your project as an absolute reproduction of the original material. If there are flaws in a project, most notably spelling, or worse, any omission of words or paragraphs, people will notice and the word will quickly spread that your site cannot be considered a trusted source for viable information. When the integrity of your operation and the credibility of the information produced by your staff are questioned by others, it is detrimental for all involved. If nobody trusts your practices and content, then your center will face problems in many areas including ridicule from faculty at your own and other institutions, spiteful letters or email from patrons, harsh criticism from your superiors, and getting turned down for grants and/or funding.

Take steps to ensure that your digitization efforts are not in vain. There are several ways you can make sure your material is as accurate as possible:

1. Use a good OCR program such as OmniPage Pro or Prime Recognition to achieve the best possible conversion from the beginning. The fewer the errors at this point, the better. This is not the place to try to save money; spend as much money as needed on the best OCR software you can afford.

2. Develop a workflow process that guarantees that the files will be proofread at least twice by two different people.

3. When you begin marking up the proofed text files in XML, it is a good idea to have the original document in front of you so you can preserve the structure of the original; for example, maintain headings, paragraphs, punctuation, italicized words, etc., and proofread the document or article a third time as you are marking it up in order to catch any mistakes or omissions that might have made it past the first two people, because this is the last stage of editing before the document goes online.

4. After you have made the XML to HTML conversion, check the HTML file in your browser to make sure everything such as headings, paragraphs, footnotes, photographs, links, and so on are working properly – it is also a good idea to glance over the text and spot check spelling, and check for special characters that are not displaying properly or are missing.

By following these few steps, you can ensure that your digitization efforts are exacting and meet the 99.95 percent accuracy goal. Remember, do not rush the proofreading process; it is a long, slow process that takes time to finish, but the rewards are well worth the time spent making sure your projects are an accurate representation of the original document.

XML markup

XML, or eXtensible Markup Language, is an essential part of the digitization of text. A W3C recommendation, XML marks up the structure of the original document, and provides an application-, platform-, and vendor-independent format that will be usable far into the future.

A brief history of markup languages

The original markup language and the ancestor of HTML and XML is SGML, or Standard Generalized Markup Language. SGML is an international standard, ISO 8879, and has been around for more than a decade. It is structural markup, which means that it marks the structural elements of a document, e.g. heading, abstract, chapter, section, subsection, and paragraph. It has long been used by industry and the military to mark up manuals for training and operations. SGML uses a DTD, or Document Type Definition, to set the rules for markup within a set of documents. The DTD specifies what tags may be used, and which tags may be used inside other tags. There are different types of DTDs for different classes of documents, and anyone can write a DTD to use for their document set. An

SGML document is useless without its DTD, because no one will know what the tags signify. An advantage of SGML is its flexibility; you can define the tags in your DTD to mark whatever aspects of the text are important for your purposes. The main drawback to SGML is its complexity. It is very difficult to learn and to use. It cannot be displayed in a web browser. Its flexibility also acts as a disadvantage, because it makes it very difficult for programmers to write software for SGML. The SGML software that is available is more expensive than most libraries can afford.

HTML, or Hypertext Markup Language, is the one with which most people are familiar. This is the language of the Web. It is a limited tag set of SGML, and it is only concerned with marking text up for layout and display. It does not preserve the structure of the document as SGML or XML do. For example, in HTML you would mark a book title with <i></i> tags so the title would be displayed in italics. In SGML or XML, the title would be marked with something like <title type="book"></title> to indicate that this phrase is a book title. HTML is flexible, forgiving and simple to use, which makes it easy for anyone to create files for the Web; however, these same attributes work against it as an archival format. To preserve the integrity of an electronic text over time, the markup language should tell us something about the structure of the document, and should adhere to certain grammatical standards. This is where XML comes in.

XML is also a child of SGML, but unlike its parent language, it has strict syntax rules. All XML documents must meet the following requirements:

- It must have a root element. This is an outer wrapper tag like the <html></html> tags that enclose an HTML document.

- Every tag must have a closing tag. SGML and HTML allow you to use an opening tag only, e.g. <p> for a paragraph. In XML the opening tag must have a matching closing tag. The <p> would require a </p>. This makes it easier to write software that acts on XML documents, because you can use the opening tag to tell the program to begin a certain function and the closing tag to tell it to cease that function.

- Tags must nest cleanly: <p><b>hi there</b></p> rather than <p><b>hi there</p></b>. Tags must close in the reverse order of that in which they opened.

- Empty tags like <br> still exist, but take a different form, <br/>, to indicate that there is no closing tag.

- All attributes must be in quotation marks: <hi rend= "italics"></hi>, not <hi rend=italics></hi>.

- Tags are case sensitive and must match exactly. The tag <bibl> could not close with the tag <Bibl>. The two tags could exist within the same document and mean entirely different things. The difference in case is enough to distinguish the tags. This is one of the toughest adjustments for those used to working in HTML, which is forgiving of tag case.

- You must declare at the top of the document that it is an XML document. The basic declaration is <?xml version= "1.0"?>.

- An XML document may or may not have a DTD. If you do use a DTD, you must declare it at the top of the document in the format: <!DOCTYPE TEI.2 SYSTEM 'teixlite.dtd'>. This declaration states the document type name, the location (in this example, on the host system), and the file name of the DTD.

An XML document must be well-formed, which means that it conforms to the requirements set out above. It may also be valid, which means that in addition to being a well-formed document, it conforms to the specifications of a Document Type Definition (DTD). To ensure that it conforms to the DTD, the XML document is validated against the DTD by a piece of software called a parser. The parser goes through the XML document, checks it against the DTD, and makes sure that all elements required by the DTD are present and that the tags are used appropriately. Common parsers include the programs SP and xmlint, which are available online as freeware. Internet Explorer can be used to check that XML files are well-formed.

XML in its raw form does not display on the Web. You must use a style sheet to render the XML document for browser viewing. IE 6.0 and higher displays XML files using cascading style sheets (CSS) like those used with HTML files. To be sure that your XML documents are viewable by all browsers, however, you must transform them into HTML using XSLT (eXtensible Stylesheet Language Transformations). XSLT is really a program written in XML that transforms the XML tags into specified HTML tags with the help of an XSLT processor such as Saxon. The Saxon software, developed by XSLT expert Michael Kay, is available for free online. There are a number of books that will be useful to you in learning XML and XSLT. Two to begin with are *The XML Bible* by

Rusty Harold (2001) and *XSLT Programmer's Reference* by Michael Kay (2001).

XML in libraries

There are two XML DTDs that are commonly used by libraries: the Encoded Archival Description (EAD) DTD and the Text Encoding Initiative (TEI) DTD. The EAD is a standard for marking up archival finding aids maintained in the Network Development and MARC Standards Office of the Library of Congress (LC) in partnership with the Society of American Archivists. It was developed by archivists and is designed to reflect the hierarchy and structure of traditional written finding aids. EAD documents have two major parts: the EAD header containing metadata about the finding aid and the <archdesc> element containing the encoded text of the finding aid itself. The header has four elements:

- <eadid> – a unique identifier for the file;
- <filedesc> – the file description, with bibliographic information about the finding aid;
- <profiledesc> – the profile description, with information about where and when the file was encoded and by whom;
- <revisiondesc> – information about any revisions to the EAD file.

The <archdesc> contains <did> elements (description identifiers) that contain sub-elements describing the containers and contents of the archival collection.

The Society of American Archivists maintains the EAD Help Pages at *http://jefferson.village.virginia.edu/ead/*. Here, you can learn about the standard, download the DTD and supporting documentation, and find information on authoring software, helper files, training opportunities offered by SAA and the University of Virginia Rare Book School, and sources for funding of EAD projects.

The Text Encoding Initiative (TEI) Guidelines are used for creating full-text resources. Developed as a cooperative project by the Association for Computing and the Humanities and the Association for Languages and Linguistic Computing, the TEI DTD preserves the structure of the text being encoded, be it novel, letter, poem, drama, diary, or journal article. It also allows encoding of names, places, dates, <keywords>, and linguistic elements. Most users find that a subset of the full TEI DTD, the TEI Lite, will meet their needs. Like the EAD, TEI documents have two basic parts: the TEI header containing metadata about the document, and the <text> element, subdivided into <front>, <body> and <back> elements, containing the encoded text of the document. The <body> is divided into <div> elements that may be defined to describe the structure of the document, whether they are chapters, sections, stanzas, or acts. The top-level <div> elements may contain additional levels of <div> elements, which may be numbered, e.g. <div1> <div2> <div3></div3></div2></div1>. While numbering of <div>s is not required, it can be very useful in keeping track of the structure of the document and avoiding encoding errors.

The TEI Consortium maintains a website at *http://www .tei-c.org* where you can find the complete guidelines, the TEI and TEI Lite DTDs, and a link to the TEI Pizza Chef, an interactive tool that lets you build your own DTD using only the TEI elements appropriate for your project. There is also information about conferences, XML tools, and the TEI-L email list.

Metadata

Metadata is simply data about data. The most familiar examples are catalog or MARC records. In digital collections, there are a number of types of metadata. Some files, including EAD, TEI, and TIFF files, contain metadata in a header that is part of the file. Other metadata schemes hold information about a file independently of the file itself. Two of the most commonly used are the Dublin Core and the Metadata Encoding and Transmission Standard (METS).

The Dublin Core was developed with input from a number of library organizations. Meetings to work out the Dublin Core Metadata Element Set were held at OCLC's headquarters in Dublin, Ohio, giving the metadata scheme its name. There are 15 elements defined in the Dublin Core, but only some are required. One aim of the Dublin Core development group was to come up with a simple, broadly applicable metadata scheme that could be implemented by organizations and projects of all sizes. There is a Dublin Core XML DTD, but Dublin core elements can also be added to HTML files in the <meta> tag or stored in a database. The Dublin Core has gained wide acceptance, largely because of its simplicity, flexibility, and applicability to materials in any format.

The Open Archives Initiative, which endeavors to build a union catalog of online collections by harvesting metadata from the collections, requires Dublin Core metadata. It was the metadata scheme adopted by the Colorado Digitization Project because it would be easy for everyone involved in the project, from academic libraries to local historical societies, to understand and use. (For more information on the Dublin Core, visit the official website at *http:// dublincore.org.*)

METS is an XML-based standard for metadata. It does not seek to replace other metadata schemes, such as Dublin Core or the TEI header, but rather to provide a structure in which to collect and reference them in an XML document. It provides for the inclusion of information about various formats and representations of digital objects, e.g. an audio file and a TEI-encoded transcript of it, and for administrative metadata such as licensing and rights information.

METS is new and not yet widely implemented, but will likely be an important metadata format for digital libraries. You can learn more about it and follow the development of the standard at the Library of Congress standards website, *http://www.loc.gov/standards/mets/*.

Databases

A database can be the best way to manage the digital objects in your collection. They can hold the metadata, image files, digital audio/video, text files, and web pages. Many websites are database driven. Databases can be searched by field or keyword, making it easy for users to find the information they need.

The best way to get a database that meets your particular needs is to design one using SQL or Oracle. This, however, requires considerable expertise and usually involves hiring an experienced programmer/database designer. Most institutions will find it easier and more cost effective to go with an out-of-the box database solution.

There are a number of powerful digital library database systems produced by well-known library software vendors. Most of these are XML-based, which is good news for migration and long-term preservation. Most are also quite expensive, although there is usually scaled pricing based on the size of the institution, and it may be possible to join together with other institutions to obtain consortium pricing.

You may also decide to go with a common database package like Microsoft Access or FileMaker® Pro. These may be adequate for the internal management of small collections, but would not be appropriate for online digital library management.

Naming and saving files

Properly naming your files is of great importance in digitization for many reasons. First, when choosing a naming convention for your files, you are setting up how each particular file will be identified, usually by volume and page number. Second, the naming convention applies to all files created from the original TIFF image, such as the text file,

XML file, and HTML file. In addition, your particular naming convention can also apply to photographs by simply adding *photo* to the end of the file name. Finally, it is important to understand that the naming convention also outlines the navigation for the files you present online.

Developing a first-rate file naming convention is an essential part in making your project work efficiently and correctly. The following is an example of how we use the file naming convention for a set of books:

1. Begin the name with a V or v – this represents volume.
2. Use the actual volume number of the set you are naming – i.e. 2, 02, 002, or 0002, depending on how many volumes are in the collection you are working with.
3. Use P or p to represent page.
4. Follow with the actual page number of the document – i.e. 1, 01, 001, or 0001, depending on how many pages are in the book.

The following is an example of what this naming convention would look like in the following areas:

- a book with 99 or fewer pages: v1p2 or v1p02;
- a book with 999 or fewer pages: v2p009; v2p025; v2p500;
- a book with 1,000 or more pages: v5p0001; v5p0010; v5p0975; v5p1250.

Important note: When using a file-naming convention that does not begin with a '0', the order of the files in your folder will not be sequential. For example, all pages that begin with a '1' are first in order, then 2, then 3, and so on. For instance, pages 1, 11–19, 100, 111–119, and so on come before any pages that begin with a 2, 3, 4, etc. So, pages 1, 11–19, 100, 111–119 and 1000 would come before page 2. When you try to arrange your files they will not arrange in sequential order. If you want to avoid that issue, all you have to do is place a '0' as the first number in the naming convention. Be sure that you place the appropriate number of zeros in front of the first number if your collection is more than 100 or 1,000 pages. This helps to keep all files in proper sequence.

You can see how you can structure a book or a set of books with this naming convention. It is important to be consistent in naming the files of each project the same way. For example, if you begin naming a volume with a capital V rather than a lower case v, be sure you begin each file name with a capital V throughout the entire project – do not ever switch between upper and lower case when naming a project's files. Think of the future: your current operating environment may not be case sensitive, but future operating systems on which you load your file may be. Be consistent to ensure your projects have as few problems as possible.

The following example was developed for naming the files of Boone Pickens' speeches. This project is unusual because it is not representative of using a volume number and pages to define the files. The convention used follows a format that is normally used when naming letters or certain types of correspondence. Instead of naming the files by a volume number or using pagination, we relied on dates and specified numbers for the different versions of the speeches. The following file-naming instructions were prepared for students working on the project.

File-Naming Steps for Scanned Pages of Pickens' Speeches

1. Enter date of speech – mmddyy

2. Enter a capital letter indicating the order in which that speech was given on the same date; for example, 'A' is for the first speech on a particular date, 'B' is for the second one given on that same date, and so on.

   *!!!*Use the order in which the files are placed *in the folder*, which do not necessarily go in order of the *times* at which the speeches were given on that date.*!!!*

   For example, if two speeches were given on October 28, 1986, one at 4:00 and another at noon, if the speech given at 4:00 comes before the one at noon in the *file folder*, the one at 4:00 would get the letter 'A', and the one at noon would get the letter 'B'.

3. Given the choices below, enter the appropriate numeral after the letter:

   1 – for the speech itself, usually done in large print, often with handwritten notes.

   2 – for press copy, usually a clean copy of the speech, done in smaller print.

   3 – other items, such as notes, points, outlines, etc.

   4, 5, etc. — use these if there is more than one draft, notes, points, and so forth for a speech.

4. End the file name with a 'p' followed by the page number of the speech. For example, if the page you just scanned is page 3 of the speech, in the filename, type p03. Remember to keep the 'p' lower case.

   The following is a sample filename of page 3 of the second speech given on October 28, 1986. This page comes from the press copy.

   Filename = 102886B2p03

After you have created your file naming convention, it is a good idea for you to document and explain the steps involved. Putting the instructions in a text document is a good idea for training purposes, but you should also include it in the header of the XML document. This is important for many reasons. First, if for any reason a text document of the file-naming structure is lost, you can easily find it in each XML document. Second, if the staff that originally created the naming convention are no longer employed at your institution and you cannot reach them to ask questions, the naming convention information is contained in the XML document's TEI header and can be retrieved, so you can see how the files are named. Finally, it is important to keep the file naming structure the same and not change it at any point during the digitization process.

Workflow

Digitizing involves several steps and many different file types are created in the process. It is easy to lose track of your progress and where you and your employees are at on a particular project if you do not have some kind of record of your progress. There might be times when you will be working on multiple projects; thus you are constantly working in several different folders, using different naming conventions, and working in different areas such as XML markup on one project and OCR'ing and proofing for another project. This could become confusing and frustrating, and take a lot of time out of your schedule searching for and finding files. It also takes time away from your schedule if you are constantly helping your employees find files and figure out what part of a project they should be working on, and it takes much needed project time and resources away from the actual project. That is why it is extremely important to develop a good workflow process, and document the progress by having a workflow log for people to use for each phase of a project.

The digitization process normally follows these steps:

1. Scanning, saving, and naming TIFF image files.
2. OCR'ing the TIFF images and naming and saving as a text file.
3. Proofreading the text file for accuracy.
4. Marking up in XML.

Figure 5.2 shows an example of a workflow log created for these steps.

Establishing good workflow procedures can make a huge difference in your center's productivity and operations. The best way to begin establishing a workflow process is to first define what needs to be done. In our case, we need to scan pages and save them as TIFF images. This should be the first step, and all pages should be scanned before starting another step. When all the pages are scanned, it is time to begin OCR'ing the images into text files. Once all pages have been OCR'd and combined into text files, it is time to begin proofreading and editing the text files for accuracy. Once that step is completed the files are ready for XML markup.

It is important for you and your staff to keep your workflow consistent and maintain the correct flow of operations. You should never skip around and do a step here or a step there. It is best to have everyone working on the same part of a project at the same time until that part is completed in order to avoid confusion. It also makes things a lot easier when answering questions and keeps everybody on the same page, so to speak.

Figure 5.2 Sample workflow log

Tiff file range scanned	OCR'd and saved as .txt	New file name	Proofed against original	XML markup
TIFF pages scanned and named according to file naming convention	*Initials/date*	*Combined all OCR'd pages from TIFF images and named for first page in the series*	*Initials/date*	*Initials/date*
Pages 01–10	DM-11-22-03	V007p001	DM-11-22-03	CA-12-01-03
Pages 11–21	DM-11-22-03	"	DM-11-22-03	CA-12-01-03
Pages 22–32	DM-11-22-03	V007p022	DM-11-23-03	DM-12-02-03
Pages 33–40	DM-11-22-03	"	DM-11-23-03	CA-12-02-03
Pages 41–56	DM-11-22-03	V007p041	DM-11-23-03	CA-12-02-03
Pages 57–65	DM-11-22-03	V007p057	DM-11-24-03	CA-12-03-03
Pages 66–72	DM-11-22-03	"	DM-11-24-03	CA-12-03-03
Pages 73–85	DM-11-22-03	V007p073	DM-11-24-03	CA-12-03-03
Pages 86–90	DM-11-22-03	V007p086	DM-11-24-03	CA-12-04-03
Pages 91–101	DM-11-22-03	V007p091	DM-11-25-03	CA-12-05-03
Pages 102–112	DM-11-22-03	V007p102	DM-11-25-03	CA-12-05-03

Putting files online

Perhaps one of the most exciting and rewarding times at your center is when you are ready to upload your files to the Internet for online viewing. Once you have created your site, uploading the files to your web server is a relatively simple task. To make sure everything is ready for online viewing, it is a good idea to check and see if all your links are linking to the proper places, that all your images and photographs are displaying properly, and that the project is completely finished. All you need to do is open the files in your browser and begin clicking on all links, footnotes, navigation bars, etc. Also, be sure and check to see if all images and photographs are displaying correctly. Once you have thoroughly checked your site for accuracy, it is time to upload your project to your web server.

When you are ready to upload your files, the first thing you need to do is make sure you have an FTP program. FTP stands for File Transfer Protocol. This is the act of transferring a file or files from your computer or server to other locations – in this case, from your computer to the web server that is hosting your website. (Refer to Chapter 3 on hardware for more information on finding an FTP program for your center.)

When using your FTP client software to upload the files to the web server the first thing you need to do is create the root directory or folder that the entire contents of the project will reside in on the web server. For this section we are using the WS_FTP program as our example. Once you have successfully opened your FTP program and logged into your web server, you are ready to begin putting your project online. The following is an example of how to use the FTP program when putting files online:

1. To create a new directory on your web server, click the *MkDir* button located on the right side of the *Remote System* dialog box, or right click inside the window and select *Make Directory* from the drop-down menu (*Note*: The *Remote System* or your web server is located on the right side of the program while your *Local System* or file server is located on the left side of the program.)

2. Type in the name of the folder you want to create and click *OK*. The folder now appears on your web server.

3. Double click the new folder you created to open the directory.

4. From the *Local System*, double click the appropriate project and its folders until you come to the folder that contains all the HTML files (*Note*: If you accidentally go too far into a folder, just click the green arrow at the top of each window to take a step back.)

5. Double click to open the folder that contains all the HTML files.

6. Click the first folder or file in the directory – it will turn blue.

7. Press and hold the *Shift* key and begin selecting all the files in the folder by clicking them with your mouse until all files are selected.

8. Press the right arrow in the middle of the program to transfer all files to the selected folder on the web server;

the files will transfer, and if you have speakers available and turned on, you will hear a video game type noise when all files have successfully transferred.

9. Click *Close* from the bottom right-hand side of the window to close the program.

Now you can go online to the URL of your project's site and see it online, and check it to make sure you have transferred everything correctly. At this point, it is also a good idea to check all links, images, and navigation online as one last measure of quality assurance.

Summary and resources

- There are several steps involved in digitization.
- Materials must go through a selection process to be considered for digitization.
- Materials must meet certain requirements before work can begin on any project.
- Steps need to be taken to preserve the original materials before, during, and after digitization.
- Know what standards are available and choose the best one for your needs.
- Set up a good file structure for your projects.
- Know what settings you should use for scanning certain materials.
- Rekeying materials is sometimes necessary.
- Use an image editing program to edit and fix image files.

- Use a good OCR software program – do not skimp on quality in this area.

- Have your text files proofread and spell-checked at least twice by two different people.

- Come up with a good file-naming system for your projects and keep the letter case consistent.

- Develop and establish a workflow process and document your progress with a workflow log.

- Upload files to your web server using FTP client software.

The following list provides details to help you locate more resources and information on digitization:

- Oklahoma State University Library Electronic Publishing Center: *http://digital.library.okstate.edu*

- Oklahoma State University Library Electronic Publishing Center Operations Manual: *http://digital.library.okstate .edu/manual/index.html*

- Colorado Digitization Program: *http://www.cdpheritage.org*

- Arts and Humanities Data Service: *http://www.ahds.ac .uk/creating/case-studies/index.htm*

- Berkeley Digital Library SunSITE: *http://sunsite.berkeley.edu*

- Cornell University Library Tutorial: *http://www.library .cornell.edu/preservation/tutorial*

- Digital Library Federation: *http://www.clir.org/diglib/ dlfhomepage.htm*

- IMLS, *A Framework of Guidance for Building Good Digital Collections*: *http://www.imls.gov/pubs/forumframework.htm*

- The NINCH Guide to Good Practice in the Digital Representation and Management of Cultural Heritage Materials: *http://www.nyu.edu/its/humanities/ninchguide*

- National Library of Australia Digitisation Policy: *http://www.nla.gov.au/policy/digitisation.html*

- Oxford Text Archive Guides to Good Practices: *http://ota.ahds.ac.uk/documents/creating*

- University of Virginia Electronic Text Center: *http://etext.lib.virginia.edu*

6

Collaboration: ways of working together

Why collaborate?

As we have discussed, digitization is a very expensive process. By collaborating with others, you can share the considerable costs of equipment, personnel, and maintenance. Collaboration is often the only way for a smaller institution to digitize its collections and make them available electronically. Grant funds make many digital projects possible, and the grant funding agencies look favorably on collaborative efforts. They consider that they are getting more for their money when the funding goes to more than one institution.

Setting considerations of money aside, working with others can produce wonderful results. One institution may hold letters or diaries of a famous person, while another has papers relating to that person's career. By collaborating on a digitization project, the institutions can reunite the dispersed collection in an online exhibit that will be of great benefit to researchers. The Online Archive of California (*http://www .oac.cdlib.org/*) allows users to search across the collections of its member institutions to find materials relating to a particular person or event. Organizations within the same region might combine forces to create online collections of holdings unique to that area. The Colorado Digitization Program (*http://www.cdpheritage.org/*) has been a leader in this type of collaborative effort. *Western Trails* (*http://www .cdpheritage.org/westerntrails/wt_collections.html*) is an ambitious new collaboration between cultural heritage institutions in Colorado, Kansas, Nebraska, and Wyoming presenting information on the great western migration in the United States. The institutions in these western states are separated by hundreds of miles – digital collaboration does not require proximity.

Ways to collaborate

There are a number of ways to work with others, ranging from the simple to the very complex. You may seek an outside consultant to work with, or enter into a partnership with another institution to put together a single project. If you get more ambitious, you may try to put together a digital consortium of institutions of various types and sizes. Which type of collaboration is appropriate depends on your situation.

Consultancy

This is the simplest form of collaboration. Your institution contracts with an expert in the field of digitization who provides services that may include advice on the purchase of hardware and software, project planning, staff training, templates for text markup, web design, and HTML conversion. Usually this person is paid, but sometimes an arrangement may be made with a university or government agency to provide advice on a pro bono basis.

Before hiring a consultant, do some research. Check with other institutions involved in digitization to get the recommendations of experts in your area. When you contact prospective consultants, request a curriculum vitae. What is the consultant's education and experience? How long have they been involved in digitization? Have they kept their skills up to date, as evidenced by continuing education seminars and training? Are the projects they have worked on similar to the project you are planning? Do they have experience with your type of institution? What are their professional affiliations? An expert in this area may have an educational background in library or information science, museum or archival studies, or the humanities. Membership and activity in a professional organization, such as the Association for Computing and the Humanities, the Society of American Archivists, the Association for Literary and Linguistic Computing or ICHIM is a good indication that skills are kept up to date. Review the consultant's publications and presentations. Do they demonstrate knowledge of the subject that will be helpful to you? Ask for references from other institutions they have assisted, especially institutions similar to your own.

Once you have decided on a consultant for the project, draw up a written agreement setting out exactly what services the consultant will provide and what fees will be charged for these services. Fees may be calculated by the hour or by the task, for example a flat fee for writing an XSLT style sheet or setting up a database. The agreement itself may take the form of a letter of agreement. It is not necessary that it be a formal contract, but it is important that both parties are very clear on what will be done and how much will be charged. Relying on a verbal agreement carries far more risk of misunderstanding and miscommunication. Getting something in writing offers more assurance of a meeting of minds. If you are applying for grant funding that will be used to pay the consulting fees, the funding agency will likely require a letter of agreement or other documentation from the proposed consultant.

Outsourcing

Outsourcing involves hiring an outside organization – either a vendor specializing in digitization or a non-profit institution with a digitization department – to carry out a digitization project for you. You may outsource only one part of a project, such as imaging or text rekeying, or you may contract with the other party to do the entire project, including hosting and maintenance. The Oklahoma State University Library Electronic Publishing Center has been involved in several such collaborations. We contracted with the Oklahoma Historical Society and the Oklahoma Academy of Science to digitize some of their scholarly publications and to host them on the OSU web server for a specified period of time. These projects included scanning the journals, converting the images to text using OCR software, marking up the articles, incorporating images of illustrations, tables, and figures, and designing the website.

As with consultants, it is important to check out a possible partner before entering into an agreement. Look at other projects they have done. This will be the best way to judge their work. You will also want to compare prices before making a decision. Once again, you should draw up a written agreement that sets out the work to be done and the prices to be charged. This agreement should specify the processes to be used, the standards to be adhered to, and the file formats and media to be provided. It should also explain how the charges will be calculated. For instance, some vendors charge by the unit or keystroke (for rekeying), while others charge by the hour. It is important to agree on a maximum price so you do not end up paying for the vendor's miscalculation of expenses.

Joint projects

In a joint project, two institutions share the labor of a digitization project. This approach is common when the institutions involved each hold portions of a major collection. By working together, they can reunite the collection online. They can also share the costs of digitization. One organization might have a high-end scanner and the ability to produce image files in TIFF, JPEG and GIF formats. The other institution could contribute OCR software and workers to perform XML markup. The resulting online collection may be hosted by one of the partners, with the other contributing funds for maintenance.

When seeking a partner for a joint project, you will likely look first at their collections. Once you have identified an institution with holdings that complement or complete your own, you can consider what assets you each might contribute to a digitization effort. One partner may only be able to contribute materials and funds while the other does the digitization work. As in the other cases, who will be responsible for what should be set out in writing. It is important to cover ownership of the digital files in the agreement. Both partners will want to keep control of the digital versions of their own holdings. Whether each will also receive copies of the other's digital files will be a matter for negotiation. You must also agree on the duration of the online project and plan an exit strategy for each partner. The Online Archive of California, although more of a consortium than a partnership, has copies of its members' agreements on its website at *http://www.oac.cdlib.org/*. These will be useful guides when drafting partnership agreements of your own.

Digital consortium

A number of institutions of various sizes and types may come together to form a digital consortium. Often such a group includes museums, libraries, archives, and historical and genealogical societies. All have something in common, most frequently region. This is the common element in the Colorado Digitization Project and the Online Archive of California. These groups are involved in ongoing projects where all members contribute materials that are digitized and accessed through a common portal. A consortium may also come together for a short-term project relating to a common theme, as in the case of the *Western Trails* project. While everyone contributes materials, some larger institutions may do more of the digitization work or provide server space for smaller institutions.

The more institutions are involved, the more complicated the management of the project will be. As always, you should begin with a written partnership agreement setting out the aims and objectives of the project, and the rights and responsibilities of each participant. The membership forms on the Online Archive of California site are a good example of this type of agreement. One institution should act as the central agent for the consortium, managing the financial resources, keeping records, and quality control.

A large-scale effort needs to employ a project manager. This person keeps track of all goals and deadlines, and ensures that all partners deliver as promised. All participants must agree on standards for scanning, file formats, metadata, markup, and accuracy, and must diligently enforce them. As the saying goes, 'The nice thing about standards is that there are so many to choose from.' The project manager's responsibilities include maintaining a record of the standards agreed upon, and acting as a reference source for participants with questions about what standard to follow.

Digital consortia often make arrangements to train participants in the various aspects of digitization. This training may be conducted at one central location, or may be available at a number of sites. It is easier to set up one central training site, but the size of the geographic area covered by the consortium may require that training be offered at a number of locations accessible to all participants. It is often the institutions in outlying areas that have the greatest need for training and the least ability to travel long distances to acquire it. The Colorado Digitization Program has set up centers around the state where participants can go for training or to use equipment and software to digitize their materials.

The consortium will also have to decide whether to handle file storage and online delivery centrally or locally. The simplest solution is to deposit all digital files with one institution that agrees to act as host for web access. This allows users to search across the collections with a minimum of technical problems. However, many institutions want to keep their files on their own server. While this is understandable, it does add to the complexity of searching across different collections. Interoperability becomes a major issue. A combined approach would keep metadata records in a central location for searching, and link them to the full records on another institution's server. There must be a portal, usually hosted by the institution acting as central agent, to allow access to the digital collections. Decentralization complicates long-term storage as well as access. If the digital collections are located on a central server, one institution takes responsibility for migrating the files and maintaining accessibility.

Other participants can contribute financially to upkeep. If, however, the files are dispersed among institutions, making sure they are maintained over time becomes far more difficult. Each institution is responsible for the files on its server, but has no control over the maintenance of files held by other institutions. As administrations, equipment, and software change, it becomes more and more likely that some files will be lost. Whether files are stored centrally or locally, it is vital to keep a complete set of backup files at a secure location.

Major collaborative projects

There are a number of successful regional, national, and international collaborations. In the United Kingdom, the Joint Information Systems Committee (JISC) sponsors the Arts and Humanities Data Service (AHDS) (*http://ahds.ac.uk/*) and the Distributed National Electronic Resource (DNER) (*http://www.jisc.ac.uk/dner/*) which promote digital collaboration, best practices, interoperability, and digital preservation. Digital preservation is a major concern of the Consortium of University Research Libraries' CURL Exemplars for Digital Archives (CEDARS) project. The UK has a national center for digital information management, UKOLN (UK Office for Library Networking), which is partly funded by the European Union. The New Opportunities Fund (*http://www.nof.org.uk/*) makes £50 million available to cultural heritage institutions for digitization projects (Allen and Bishoff, 2002). The European Union is making long-term plans for digital collaborations between memory institutions. The National Libraries of Australia, Canada, and Denmark have taken leading roles in fostering digitization collaborations in their countries (Allen and Bishoff, 2002).

In the United States, the Library of Congress set digital collaboration in motion with its *American Memory* project, which has resulted in over 7 million images of cultural artifacts becoming available online. The University of Michigan and Cornell University collaborate on the *Making of America* project, and have issued reports on the various stages of the project that are helpful to those considering a collaborative project. The Institute for Museum and Library

Services (IMLS) and the National Science Foundation are US government agencies with a major focus on funding digitization efforts. The IMLS has funding specifically earmarked for collaborations between institutions. One of its great success stories is the Colorado Digitization Project, which has set the standard for digital collaborations between memory institutions of varying types and sizes. In addition to developing a website where the collections can be accessed (hosted by the Colorado Alliance of Research Libraries), setting standards for scanning and metadata that are observed by all participants, and maintaining a union catalog of metadata for searching across collections, the CDP provides regional scanning centers, training, and project funding. They provide a section on Digitization Resources for cultural heritage institutions on their website at *http://www .cdpheritage.org/resource/introduction/* to assist others who are trying to get a collaborative project off the ground.

Challenges

While there are many benefits to collaborating, there are difficulties as well. As anyone who has ever served on a committee knows, conflicts will arise whenever people come together to accomplish a common purpose. Libraries have a long history of inter-institutional collaboration, and share a common professional vocabulary and standards for describing and displaying information. However, when libraries begin working with museums, archives, historical societies, or other libraries of very different types (school, special, small public libraries), differences will emerge. Nancy Allen and Liz Bishoff of the Colorado Digitization Project identify the major issues that arise:

- metadata and interoperability;
- scanning and presentation of images;
- security;
- rights management and legal issues;
- digital archiving (Allen and Bishoff, 2002).

Metadata in libraries include Dublin Core, MARC records, and Encoded Archival Description (EAD). It is intended to assist users in finding the information they seek. Museums use discipline-specific metadata intended only for the use of staff. Librarians are oriented to providing free access to information, while curators and archivists often must protect their holdings by severely restricting access.

This difference in organizational cultures raises issues in the areas of security and scanning and presenting images online. Sometimes museums do not want everyone to be aware of their valuable holdings, and they need to guard their rights to images that are sources of income. If anyone can download a high-quality image of one of their paintings, there is a real danger that some of these users will use the image in inappropriate or illegal ways. The holdings of libraries tend to have less aesthetic value, and librarians are eager to make high-quality images available to researchers. Some projects employ watermarks to protect images, while others use low resolution on images that might be misused. Rights management also comes into play here. The rights to a photograph may be owned by the photographer rather than by the institution that holds the picture. Digital rights to museum holdings are often determined by a deed of gift, while libraries are more likely to be concerned with copyright issues.

Guidelines for working together

What are the rules for a successful collaboration? Michael Schrage (1995) lists the following requirements:

- competence;
- mutual respect, tolerance, and trust;
- a shared, mutually understood goal;
- a focus on strengths;
- shared resources;
- communication;
- clear line of responsibility, without restrictive boundaries;
- not all decisions need to be made by consensus;
- physical presence is unnecessary;
- effective use of outside experts and assistance.

NINCH enumerates guidelines for working with others on digitization projects in its *Guide to Good Practice in the Digital Representation and Management of Cultural Heritage Materials* (*http://www.nyu.edu/its/humanities/ninchguide/*):

- Look for a strategic fit when selecting collaborators. Find partners who have collections that complement your own and/or resources that you do not have.

- Commit to *equal* participation in shaping projects and sharing the benefits.

- Involve all partners in all stages.

- Establish clear lines of communication, and document all communication.

- Moderate and manage expectations, including those of donors and funders.

- Adopt shared project goals and focus. Create a mission statement or other documentation of your goals.

- Establish a steering committee whose make-up reflects that of the project participants. There should be representatives from all types of institutions involved, and from organizations of various sizes and geographic location. It is also a good idea to include representatives of the user community, at least in an advisory capacity.

- Do not amplify institutional hesitation. Act – do not just talk.

- Have the flexibility to accommodate the different aims, structures, and needs of partners.

- Document areas of responsibility, and track everyone's progress.

- Ensure accountability. All participants must live up to their commitments if the project is going to work. Have one person (project manager) to enforce milestones and timelines.

- Embed interoperability.

- Cement collaboration with face-to-face meetings. Keep minutes and formal agreements. There is a good reason for getting things in writing: it prevents misunderstandings.

- Pool your resources.

- Avoid duplication of effort.

- Trust and respect your collaborators. If you cannot, you probably should not be working with them. Try to understand their organizational culture and professional skills.

- Ensure equity of access to and benefits of the final product.

- Ensure that partners have compatible exit strategies. Make sure it does not all fall apart if one party needs to withdraw.

Summary and resources

- Collaboration allows institutions to share resources, personnel, and equipment.

- You can reunite dispersed collections, increase awareness of holdings, and improve access to collections by working with others whose collections complement your own.

- Funding agencies look favorably on collaborations, and some, such as IMLS, actively encourage them.

- Using a consultant is the simplest way of working with someone outside your institution. Check the expert's background and get recommendations before employing a consultant.

- You may outsource by hiring a vendor or by contracting with a non-profit agency to digitize your materials for you.

- A joint project involves two partners who hold parts of a dispersed collection, or complementary collections.

- A digital consortium is the largest and most complex type of collaboration. It may involve institutions of different types and sizes, and is often defined by a geographic area – state, region, or country.

- The partners to a collaborative project may bring different things to the table. Some will only contribute materials, while others will provide equipment, personnel, software, training, or digitization services.

- All types of collaboration require some sort of written agreement between the parties to spell out everyone's rights and responsibilities.

- Collaboration involves challenges as well as benefits. Areas where problems arise include metadata, interoperability, scanning and presentation of images, security, rights management, and digital archiving. The difference in organizational cultures of the project partners is behind many of these conflicts.

- Working together effectively requires commitment to a common goal, accountability, mutual respect, flexibility, and communication.

Books and articles

- Allen, Nancy and Bishoff, Liz (2002) 'Collaborative digitization: libraries and museums working together,' *Advances in Librarianship*, 26: 43–81.

- Schrage, Michael (1995) 'The rules of collaboration,' *Forbes ASAP Supplement*, 5 June: 88–9.

Online resources

- Arts and Humanities Data Service: *http://ahds.ac.uk/*
- California Digital Library: *http://www.cdlib.org*
- Colorado Digitization Project: *http://www.cdpheritage.org*
- Consortium of Research Libraries CEDARS Project: *http://www.leeds.ac.uk/cedars/*
- Distributed National Electronic Resource: *http://www.jisc.ac.uk/dner/*
- Institute of Museum and Library Services: *http://www.imls.gov*
- National Library of Australia: *http://www.nla.gov.au/padi/*
- National Library of Canada: *http://www.nlc-bnc.ca/*
- National Science Foundation Digital Library Initiative: *http://dli2nsf.gov*
- New Opportunities Fund: *http://www.nof.org.uk/*
- The NINCH Guide to Good Practice in the Digital Representation and Management of Cultural Heritage Materials: *http://www.nyu.edu/its/humanities/ninchguide/*
- Online Archive of California: *http://www.oac.cdlib.org/*
- UKOLN: *http://www.ukoln.ac.uk/*

7

Funding

Money – it is the sine qua non for every digitization project. Finding the money can be a challenge. Digitization is an expensive undertaking; there are limited funds available from public and private sources, and there is competition for those funds. In this chapter we will look at the types of costs that you will incur in a digitization project and the ways you can pay for them.

Digitization costs

The costs you will encounter fall into three categories:

1. *Technology and workflow costs.* This category includes computers, scanners, other equipment, software, training, and staffing costs. This is the area where ramp-up costs hit you hard. The first project is the most expensive because of the initial investment in equipment, software, and training. Once an infrastructure is in place, staffing will be the primary expense on any project, although there will be necessary expenditures on upgrades to equipment and software and updates to training, and the occasional capital investment for special equipment. Workflow costs vary from project to project, depending on what types of materials you are digitizing, and at what level. Scanning

images of unbound pages at a lower resolution is less time consuming and less expensive than digitizing a bound book, which is scanned at a high resolution, OCR'd, and marked up in XML. Labor costs in your area also impact your workflow costs.

2. *Intellectual property costs.* The costs of determining and obtaining rights to digitize materials can be considerable and, in some cases, prohibitive. As expensive as it may be to obtain legal rights to publish online, failure to get this clearance will be far more costly. Penalties for violating intellectual property rights are severe, and it is never a good idea to take a chance and digitize a work whose legal status is unclear. Intellectual property costs include the time spent determining the copyright status of materials, tracking down the rights holder, and negotiating terms as well as the royalties that must be paid. The simplest way to minimize these costs is to choose works that are clearly in the public domain.

3. *Institutional costs.* The technological infrastructure to support a digitization effort is an ongoing expense for the institution. Digitization must be included in the overall planning for capital expenditures. Institutional commitment at the highest level is necessary for long-term survival of digitization programs.

Estimating costs

An accurate estimate of costs is essential. There are a number of studies of the price of digitization that can act as guides. The University of Michigan did a cost study of the *Making of*

America IV project, tracking the costs of retrieving volumes from storage, identifying and repairing books, disbanding volumes and shipping to vendors for rekeying, scanning, metadata creation, OCR and markup, and quality control. The cost per page worked out to be 20–27 cents. This was, however, only a range based on a hypothetical most productive month when everyone was at their most efficient. The greatest factor in keeping costs down was the volume of the project. Economies of scale are the way to keep costs down. For smaller institutions, these can be achieved through collaboration. The initial ramp-up costs were the most expensive and the most difficult part of the project.

Steven Puglia of the National Archives and Records Administration recently updated his 1999 study 'The costs of digital imaging' at the NINCH symposium on the Price of Digitization. He reviewed several projects and drew from his experience as a reviewer of grant applications. He found that on average one-third of the costs of a digital project can be attributed to digital conversion, with slightly more than one-third going to metadata creation and cataloging and slightly less than one-third for administration and quality control. Costs from projects at the Library of Congress National Digital Library Program, the Denver Public Library, and the Corbis Bettman Archive put the price of creating a single digital image at $20. The Virginia Historical Inventory spent an average of $24.45 per item, although maps cost $109 to digitize. The costs reported for digitizing books ranged from $292 to $2,500.

This brings up a problem discussed by Stuart Lee in his 2001 article 'Digitization: is it worth it?' The cost of digitizing varies widely depending on what materials you are converting. In other words, your mileage may vary. While studies may serve to provide a benchmark for digitizing materials of a certain type, the best way to come up with an accurate estimate of costs for your project is to do a test run. Take a sample of the materials you plan to digitize and take them through the process of scanning, metadata creation, OCR, image editing, proofreading, and text markup.

It is important to select a sample that is representative of all the material. A cautionary tale follows. When the Electronic Publishing Center was preparing to digitize the *Proceedings* of the Oklahoma Academy of Science, we chose a volume at random for a test run. The *Proceedings* publishes articles from all scientific disciplines, from botany and biology to chemistry, physics, and mathematics, and these can vary widely in content and in the challenges they pose to digitization. We were scanning the articles and then converting them to electronic text using OCR. The OCR software read the text well enough, but had difficulties with italics, numerical formulas, chemical symbols, and Greek letters. The articles in the volume we chose dealt primarily with subjects in the life sciences – biology, botany, and zoology. These particular articles contained numerous Latin scientific names for species of plants and animals that were printed in italics. In addition, these articles required cleanup during the proofreading process, but it did not slow down the process to any great extent. Unfortunately, there were no chemistry or physics articles in the volume, a fact that did not register with our staff of humanities majors. We based our estimated costs on the test run and received funding from the Oklahoma Academy of Science. When we began the actual project, we quickly ran into problems with the articles containing chemical formulas, mathematical equations, and Greek letters. The OCR software handled the articles in unpredictable ways, which slowed down the proofreading process considerably. Because the text files needed to be in ASCII format for markup, there was no straightforward way to designate the special features. Greek letters were spelled out by name, e.g. alpha, and the person doing markup had to watch carefully for these and insert the appropriate special character code. Chemical formulas had to be marked for superscript and subscript characters, which usually required referring back to the print article. Math articles had to be re-keyed as the OCR was incapable of handling the numerical formulas. All of these problems caused the digitization to take longer and cost more than anticipated. The moral of this story is this: know your material, and the special characteristics that must be considered in the digitization process.

Outsourcing

After doing a test run, you should consider whether it would be cheaper to outsource some of the process. There are a number of companies that scan images, rekey text, and even do XML markup. Charges for rekeying are about 60–70 cents per thousand keystrokes. At 2,000–2,500 keystrokes per page, this works out to $2.00–$2.50 per page. It should never cost more to convert text than to send it to a vendor to be rekeyed. There are also companies who specialize in producing high-quality digital images. If you have a project that requires special equipment, such as maps that need an oversize scanner, a vendor can provide that service for far less than the capital investment in new equipment. Any vendor you work with will need to know the nature of the project, a general description of the materials involved, the objective of the project, where the work is to be performed, and the schedule for completion. The type of individual items, the number of items to be digitized, the size of the objects, the size of the image files, and handling specifications will all have an impact on the quoted price. When looking for a vendor, be sure to ask for references, and try to determine if the vendor has worked on a project similar to yours.

Hidden costs

Some costs are overlooked when estimating the price of digitization. These include the care and feeding of what you create: the storage, migration, cataloging, archiving, and training costs. Steven Puglia (1999) found that maintenance costs for the first ten years after the creation of a digital collection will be 50–100 percent of the initial investment, though the use of a larger repository could drop this cost to 10–25 per cent. Network infrastructure costs, including installation, staffing, and maintenance for ten years, is five times the initial investment. Costs for the full lifecycle of information technology run at ten times the development costs.

Stephen Chapman of Harvard has studied the preservation costs for digital collections and has found that there is a dearth of affordable repository storage. This is a problem because most creators of digital content need to use a storage repository to provide insurance against file degradation and obsolescence, system failure, technology changes, and loss of usability. In comparing costs for the storage of books and the storage of archival quality digital files, Chapman found that the cost of storing the same amount of information, i.e. a given number of books, was nine times greater for the digital version. Cost differences were even more dramatic for multimedia files. The storage of digital audio and video was up to 116 times the price of storing the tapes. Digital repositories charge by the gigabyte, so larger files are more expensive. ASCII text files, which would include those marked up in XML, are the least expensive digital objects to store. If digital repositories are not affordable, consumers will not use them, putting vast amounts of digital information at risk of loss. He presented his findings at the NINCH symposium on the Price of Digitization in Spring 2003.

Funding sources

Where will you get the funds to pay for your digitization project? The basic sources of money are cost recovery via sales or subscriptions, grant funding, and institutional support. Each of these has its advantages and its limits.

Grants

Grant funding is the way most digitization projects get their start. A number of private foundations and government entities provide grant money for digital projects – the National Endowment for the Humanities, the Institute for Museum and

Library Services, and the National Science Foundation in the United States, and the Arts and Humanities Research Board in the United Kingdom are some of the agencies that support digitization projects. Grant funding can be invaluable when getting started in digitization, but it eventually becomes a hamster wheel where you are constantly chasing new grant funds. Given the complexity of grant applications, a small institution without a full-time grant writer could not keep up with the demands of constant grant seeking. Collaboration can be a way to alleviate the toll constant fund-raising takes on an organization. Once again, the shared load is a lighter load.

When applying for grants, you must first be able to assure the grant-funding agency to which you are applying that you have the rights to do what you are proposing, i.e. that you have copyright clearance on the materials in question. Next you will need to prove the value of what you are proposing and that your methodology is correct. Both components must be present if you are to win the grant. Make sure the reviewer understands why you are the right institution to do this project; you cannot assume they will know you have the definitive collection in the subject area.

The basic format for a grant is an overview of the project, an executive summary, a budget, and a detailed description of the proposal. It is important to be specific about the scope, the standards you plan to use, and the benefits to potential users. Follow the grant application guidelines to the letter. Write clearly, and do not be afraid that you are patronizing the reviewer by explaining everything in detail. It is far more likely – and more detrimental – that you will not tell the reviewers enough about the project. Make the project sound exciting. If you do not sound enthusiastic about the project, it will be hard to inspire someone to give you money. It can be helpful to do a mock-up site that will demonstrate what you have in mind. Try to work with the program officers; they can be invaluable sources of information and guidance. It is a bad idea to submit a grant application without first contacting someone at the funding agency to make sure what you are proposing is something they would be interested in funding.

Cost recovery

The difficulty of continuing digital projects while constantly chasing grant funds has led some institutions to investigate ways of making their projects self-supporting. This means charging users in some way for access to their digitized materials. Many charge for hard copies of the images on their sites, and others have set up subscription services, which allow users to access the site for a set fee. Some have entered into agreements with publishing companies to market their digital collections. Any of these efforts requires accounting, billing, and marketing functions. In addition to requiring unfamiliar tasks, charging for access to information goes against traditional library culture with its ethic of free access to information for all. Whether models can be developed that allow producers of digital content to make their projects self-sustaining remains to be seen.

Institutional support

Institutional support is essential for any digitization project. Without it, the long-term viability of the digital collection would be in serious doubt. There must be a commitment to digitization from the highest levels of the organization if the program is to endure and grow. Current budget difficulties have made it more difficult for institutions to be as supportive as they might wish. There will always be competition for funds within any organization, and digital programs must establish themselves as a key part of the institution's mission if they are to be a budget priority. This means educating the decision-makers at the highest levels about the benefits that accrue to the organization from producing digital collections, as well as the benefits conferred on users. Digitization projects can do a great deal to raise the profile of an organization and its holdings, and result in positive publicity, especially if they are marketed effectively. You cannot expect the powers that be in your establishment to instantly recognize the value of a digitization program. You must get out and promote your online efforts, through articles, news releases, and presentations at conferences, and bring recognition to your organization's efforts to contribute to global information resources. Administrators like projects that reflect well on their organization and are more likely to support them. Promoting your work within your institution and in the professional and educational community will pay off in stronger institutional support.

Summary and resources

- Digitization costs fall into three categories: technology and workflow costs, intellectual property costs, and institutional costs.

- Technology and workflow costs cover your investment in equipment, software, staff, quality control, and training costs.

- Intellectual property costs can be the most prohibitive. They include determining the copyright status of a work, tracking down the copyright holder, and negotiating payment for digitization rights.

- Institutional costs are those that must be absorbed by the host institution, and include the technical infrastructure and the long-term preservation of digital resources.

- An accurate estimate of costs is essential before you can seek funding. There are a number of online reports that can act as benchmarks, but the most reliable method is to do a test run of a representative sample of the materials to be digitized.

- After estimating what it would cost to digitize in-house, check the price of outsourcing some of the work; it should never cost more to convert text than to send it to a vendor to be rekeyed.

- The hidden costs of digitization are storage, maintenance, and preservation. Do not forget to consider these when pricing your project. They can range from 50–100 percent of the initial investment.

- Grant funding is the major source of support for most digitization projects. However, competition for grant money is fierce, and you run the risk of getting caught on the grant-chasing hamster wheel, spending most of your time seeking new funding.

- Some institutions are experimenting with cost recovery models. There is no definitive model at this time for self-sustaining projects, but there is agreement that for long-term survival, cultural and educational institutions will need to figure out some way to support their projects that does not depend on government or foundation funding.

- Institutional support is essential for the long-term survival of digitization programs. You must sell your organization's administrators on the value of digital projects to the institution's mission. Promote your projects both within the organization and to the community at large.

Articles

- Chapman, Stephen (2003) 'Counting the costs of digital preservation: is repository storage affordable?', *Journal of Digital Information*, 4 (2): Article No. 178. Available at *http://jodi.ecs.soton.ac.uk/Articles/v04/i02/Chapman/chapman-final.pdf.*

- Lee, Stuart (2001) 'Digitization: is it worth it?', *Computers in Libraries*, 21 (5): 28–32.

Online resources

- Arts and Humanities Research Board (AHRB): *http://www.ahrb.ac.uk/*

- Arts and Humanities Data Service (AHDS): information for those applying for AHRB awards: *http://ahds.ac.uk/ahrb/index.htm*

- Colorado Digitization Program: Funding Resources: *http://www.cdpheritage.org/resource/funding/rsrc _funding.html*

- Digital Libraries Initiative Phase 2: *http://www.dli2 .nsf.gov/*

- Foundation Center: *http://www.fdncenter.org/*

- Hughes, Lorna (2003) Report on *The Price of Digitization: New Cost Models for Cultural and Education Institutions.* Paper at the Digitization Symposium presented by NINCH and Innodata, New York City, 8 April: *http://www.ninch .org/forum/price.report.html*

- Institute for Museum and Library Services: *http://www .imls.gov*

- National Endowment for the Humanities: *http://www .neh.gov*

- Puglia, Steven (1999) 'The costs of digitization', *RLG DigiNews*, 3 (5): *http://www.rlg.org/preserv/diginews*

- *Technology Grant News*: *http://www.technologygrantnews .com/*

8

Putting collections online

Website design

When it comes to website design, perhaps the single most important aspect to consider when developing your site is navigation, navigation, navigation. One of the biggest faults of many websites is the difficulty in finding exactly what you are looking for on a particular website. If your website is difficult to navigate, many people who visit your site will quickly lose interest or become so frustrated trying to find a particular document or piece of information that they will not return to your site, or they might send you negative comments about your site. However, if you do receive negative comments about your site or a particular project's site, use that information constructively to make changes or implement those suggestions to make your online audience appreciate your efforts and collections. If possible, reply to feedback by thanking the person for the suggestions and letting him or her know what actions, if any, you are taking to make the next visit more enjoyable. If you happen to receive positive comments about your site, use that information constructively as well.

Your goal should be to make your site aesthetically pleasing to the visitor while offering and maintaining a scholarly ethos. Providing straightforward site navigation is a must, and it should provide information pertaining to all areas of your center and institution.

Design basics

Before you begin designing your site, you must know who your audience is, why they will need to use your site, and the context in which they will use your site. Audience, purpose, and context are the basics for designing any type of document, including a website. Ask yourself who the audience of the site will be. Will it be used by school children? Hobbyists? Scholars and professional researchers? Educators? A combination of all of these? Each of these audiences has needs and expectations that must be met if they are to be satisfied with their experience of your website. Decide first who your primary audience is and design your main page for them. You may decide to design separate access pages for elementary or secondary school students and teachers, or a more advanced search page for scholars. To find out what an audience needs, you have to ask them. Talk to schoolteachers and librarians about the needs of their users. Talk to kids. Interview scholars in the subject area your site will cover. The needs and expectations of scientists, historians, and linguists will vary.

Once you have determined the primary and secondary audiences for your site, think about the purpose of it. Why will your audience use your site and what will they use it for? Make sure your design will let them find what they need to fulfill their purpose for visiting the website in the first place. When you know why your users are coming to your website, consider how they will access it. What will be the context in which they come to the site? Will it be used primarily by academics who have fast broadband connections? Will it be used by a population that has access to the Web only over low-speed, dial-up connections? You do not want to make your site inaccessible to your primary audience by using large image files, Flash™, or multimedia elements that they do not have the bandwidth to handle. Also, if you are designing for scholars and serious researchers, you want to avoid making your site too flashy, frivolous or commercial in appearance. Think of the difference between academic journals and glossy magazines. You want your site to have the gravitas to make an academic audience take it seriously. Similarly, a site designed primarily for schoolchildren will need to be livelier and more interactive than one designed for scholars. Knowing your audience and their needs will guide your entire design process.

When you begin creating your site, you should first draw a few thumbnail sketches of your initial layout. This method allows you to plan out your site using a much more sophisticated approach instead of initially opening an HTML editor and using it to design, plan, and layout your site. When you are thinking up ideas of how you want your site to look, put them down on paper and draw out your initial concept. This provides you with something to visually assist you in designing, and prevents you from forgetting a certain area that you might not remember if too much time passes, or if you have trouble remembering and do not want to lose your ideas. Once you have sketched out and put your design ideas on paper, it is time to begin the actual construction of your website. The following elements of web page design are what we generally use when creating our website collections. These elements can provide you with helpful and useful information when you begin creating your website.

HTML

In order to create a web page you need to know or have a good understanding of HTML and how it works. In addition, you need to know what programs are available to assist you with web page creation. The useful thing about HTML is that it can be created with a simple text editor such as Notepad. All you need to know is how to code documents in HTML. However, there are much better tools available to help you create HTML. Microsoft Office FrontPage and Macromedia Dreamweaver are two programs that allow you to visually construct your web pages rather than coding them by hand. There are also shareware and freeware HTML editing tools such as Arachnophilia© and HotDog©, which are text-based editors, but provide many more options and tools than a plain text editor.

Depending on your skill level and familiarity with HTML, it might be a good idea to pick up a book on HTML. HTML books and tutorials are a great way to learn about HTML. These books contain all the information you need to know about writing HTML and usually contain step-by-step instructions on how to do certain tasks. Elizabeth Castro's *HTML for the World Wide Web* (2003) is an excellent book designed for beginners and professionals alike.

Usability, navigation and navigation bar

As mentioned earlier, navigation is perhaps the most important aspect of usability when designing an effective website. Users must be able to browse the contents of your website easily and be able to navigate back to a project's homepage and the center's homepage. The top, bottom, or side of a web page are the best places to put links for navigation. One way to ensure proper accessibility is with a navigation bar. The navigation bar is the most important part of the web page when referring to usability. Having a navigation bar on your center's main website is a must. This allows your online community to access not only your project's web pages, but your entire center's website as well. The navigation bar should include all the pages that make up your center's entire site. If you do not put your projects in the navigation bar, be sure your online audience can access the projects from your center's homepage. Navigation bars can be placed anywhere on a web page, but they generally look and work best on the left side or top of a web page. Navigation bars consist of links, and can be designed in many different ways. For example, the main navigation bar for the OSU Library EPC resides on the left-hand side of our web pages, and consists of bulleted text links to our projects and other EPC-related web pages (see Figure 8.1).

Many navigation bars are made up of bulleted text links, icons, or images. Remember, without proper site navigation your site will not appeal to the online community, and your projects might not have the impact they could if only they were easier to browse.

| Figure 8.1 | EPC homepage with left-hand side navigation bar |

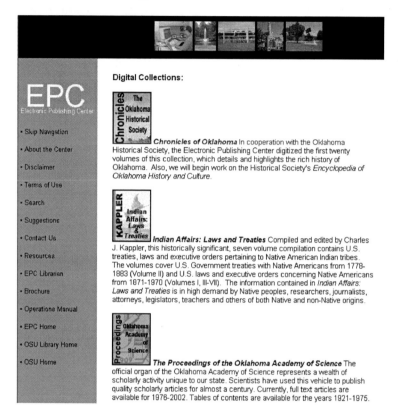

Digital Collections:

Chronicles of Oklahoma In cooperation with the Oklahoma Historical Society, the Electronic Publishing Center digitized the first twenty volumes of this collection, which details and highlights the rich history of Oklahoma. Also, we will begin work on the Historical Society's *Encyclopedia of Oklahoma History and Culture*.

Indian Affairs: Laws and Treaties Compiled and edited by Charles J. Kappler, this historically significant, seven volume compilation contains U.S. treaties, laws and executive orders pertaining to Native American Indian tribes. The volumes cover U.S. Government treaties with Native Americans from 1778-1883 (Volume II) and U.S. laws and executive orders concerning Native Americans from 1871-1970 (Volumes I, III-VII). The information contained in *Indian Affairs: Laws and Treaties* is in high demand by Native peoples, researchers, journalists, attorneys, legislators, teachers and others of both Native and non-Native origins.

The Proceedings of the Oklahoma Academy of Science The official organ of the Oklahoma Academy of Science represents a wealth of scholarly activity unique to our state. Scientists have used this vehicle to publish quality scholarly articles for almost a century. Currently, full text articles are available for 1976-2002. Tables of contents are available for the years 1921-1975.

Making sure your online audience can find information quickly and with as few clicks as possible is an essential part of usability and navigation, especially if you want your projects to have as much exposure and potential as they possibly can. Straightforward site navigation with links that allow users to easily explore and backtrack within your site can provide them with a wonderful online experience.

Cascading style sheets

Cascading style sheets, or CSS for short, are an indispensable part of website design. Cascading style sheets contain all the stylistic information about your web pages. Instead of specifying what each tag represents in all of your web pages, let the CSS do it for you. The CSS works by creating a style sheet that contains all the stylistic choices for each tag represented in an HTML document. For example, you might want each paragraph to use the Arial font. So, in the cascading style sheet you would specify that all paragraphs (<p></p> tags) use the Arial font. You can see how you are able to control how the page is viewed when it is accessed by all who visit your site. Figure 8.2 provides an example of a cascading style sheet.

The style sheet is a separate file that resides on your web server within a project's folder. The CSS is called on by the HTML document to display the information. In order to be able to use style sheets, you need to enter a line in each HTML document that specifies where to call it from. The style sheet information is located in the heading or <head> tag within the web page. The following is an example of what the code for linking to a style sheet looks like in the heading of an HTML document:

```
<LINK  REL="stylesheet"  TYPE="text/css"  HREF="styles.css"
MEDIA="screen">
```

Cascading style sheets are an excellent way to ensure a consistent look for your web pages, and they also preserve the way your web pages are meant to be viewed when people using different computers or browsers view your pages.

Figure 8.2   **Example of a cascading style sheet.**

```
.sup {position:relative; top:-20; left: -5}
.sub {position:relative; top: 20; left: 9}
.sub2 {position:relative; top: 20; left: 20}
.margin {margin-left: 40px;   margin-right: 40px; font-family:
    "arial", "verdana", "geneva"; font-size: 15px}
.total {border-bottom:double}
.smallfont {font-family: "arial", "verdana", "geneva"; font-size:
    13px; margin-left: 30px}
.sup2 {position:relative; top: -5; left: -6}
.line {position: relative; left: -6px}
p {font-size: 15px; font-family: "arial", "verdana", "geneva";
    line-height: 19px}
ol {font-family: "arial", "verdana", "geneva"; font-size: 15px;
    margin-left: 40px; margin-right: 40px}
H2 {margin-right:  40px;   font-family: "arial", "verdana",
    "geneva"}
H3 {margin-right:  40px;   font-family: "arial", "verdana",
    "geneva"}
H4 {margin-right:  40px;   font-family: "arial", "verdana",
    "geneva"}
th {font-family: "arial", "verdana", "geneva"}
dl {font-family: "arial", "verdana", "geneva"; font-size: 14px;
    margin-left: 40px; margin-right: 40px}
td {font-family: "arial", "verdana", "geneva"}
sup {font-family: "arial", "verdana", "geneva"; font-size: 12px}
sub {font-family: "arial", "verdana", "geneva"; font-size: 12px}
.footnote {font-family: "arial", "verdana", "geneva"; font-size:
    14px;  margin-left: 110px;  margin-right: 90px;}
UL {margin-left: 40px;   margin-right: 40px; font-size: 15px;
    font-family: "arial", "verdana", "geneva"; line-height: 19px}
```

Images

Images are an attractive way to enhance the visual appeal of your websites. Images provide a good aesthetic touch to your site as long as they are placed correctly within the web pages and are not too large in terms of actual picture and file size. Images for photographic display should be in the JPEG image format. The JPEG is intended to provide good quality photographic results while maintaining a relatively small file size. When using photographs for a website make sure they are in the JPEG format.

Sometimes you might use buttons for your links rather than plain text links. If so, you would probably want to opt for the GIF file format. GIF files are small in size like the JPEG, but the main difference between the two is the amount of colors a GIF is capable of displaying. JPEG files can display millions of colors; however, the GIF is limited to 256. The GIF image format is useful for when you want to use images that do not have white space around them so that it blends in seamlessly with the background of the web page.

Accessibility guidelines

Signed into law in 1990, the Americans with Disabilities Act (ADA) was created to promote universal accessibility for disabled persons, and to prevent discrimination against those who have disabilities. Section 508 of the ADA covers accessibility guidelines for web pages. Some commonly used elements of websites – images, links, frames, Flash – can pose serious barriers for those with disabilities. The blind use reader/browsers that read the contents of a website to them. These special browsers cannot interpret images unless you provide a text description, or *alt* element within the image tag. Users who are unable to use a mouse because of paralysis or other physical limitations need to be able to navigate your site by using the *Tab* key to move between links.

A text-only website that contains no images, animation or multimedia elements is one alternative to having an ADA compliant website. However, this is a time-consuming solution because you are responsible for maintaining two separate sites. With a little education about ADA guidelines, you can create a fully ADA-compliant website complete with graphics and other aesthetic additions, and not have to rely on a separate text-only site. To make sure that your site is accessible, you can use a free testing tool called Bobby™, available at *http://bobby .watchfire.com/bobby/html/en/index.jsp*.

Alt, height *and* width *tags*

However, as we mentioned earlier, there are alternatives to having and maintaining two separate websites. You can have a website that displays graphics and still be ADA compliant. The use of *alt* in an image tag provides descriptive text about what the photo contains. For example, a normal image tag looks like this:

```
<img src="images/v007p034photo.jpg">
```

This displays the image onscreen and allows users to view it. However, if people have graphics turned off or use a text-only browser, then there is no indication that an image exists or what the contents of the image represent. When you add *alt* into the image tag and place a text-based description with it, you are enabling people who have images disabled or text-only browsers to see what the image is or about. The following is an example of using *alt* to describe the contents of an online image:

```
<img src="images/v007p034photo.jpg" alt="Photo of
Black Mesa">
```

The *alt* tag displays what the image is and provides a text-based description of the contents. This allows users who cannot display graphics in their browser to have a text-based description of the contents of the image. In addition, it is a good idea to include the height and width of the image as well as the *alt* tag. So, your image tags would look like the following:

```
<img src="images/v007p034photo.jpg" width="100"
height="160" alt="Photo of Black Mesa">
```

Avoid using frames

Frames are not accessibility friendly. First, you must have a browser that supports frames. Second, not all the information is contained on one page. Finally, some frames follow you when you exit the site, and you must use a keystroke or close your browser to get rid of them. Frames can be useful and an attractive addition to a website, but if you are going to use frames, you need to maintain a separate non-frames version, too.

Publicizing your website

You need to make sure your audience and the major search engines know your site is online. Search engines have links that let you submit your site to them so it will be included when they search the Web. The best search engines will find you anyway using their spiders (an indexing tool that scans your pages from top to bottom in order to register the content in a search engine), but they will find you sooner if you submit your site to them. You will receive e-mail offers to register your site with search engines. It is not worth spending the money for these services when it is simpler to register your site with the major engines yourself. Save those funds for another purpose.

To inform your potential audience of the debut of your site, you can issue press releases to newsletters or journals in the field, and post announcements on e-mail discussion lists. Presentations at professional conferences give you the opportunity to demonstrate your site to potential users. Articles for professional journals also provide a forum for describing and promoting your site. The website is an electronic resource to be included in your library's online catalog. If you are a member of a cooperative like OCLC, you can submit the catalog record for the site to their union catalog. Some organizations, like the Association of Research Libraries and the Text Encoding Initiative Consortium maintain online registries of digital projects. You can fill out online forms to register your site with these lists.

Keeping statistics

When the users do start to come, you need to keep statistics on the number of visits your site receives. These numbers can be used to justify the expense of creating and maintaining the site, to prove the value of what you are doing to your administration, and to evaluate the success of your site. Funding agencies frequently require such evaluations. To acquire the statistics for hits on your website, work with your information technology staff. They may already have software installed that keeps track of hits that can be broken down by time period, area of the website visited, and length of average visit. If they are unable to assist you, you can download free webcounters that will record hits on your site. Statistics can also provide useful feedback for you. If the usage is unexpectedly low, consider additional ways to promote and publicize your site. If the length of the average visit is not what you expected, you might analyze the navigability of the site to determine if users are getting frustrated and leaving.

Summary and resources

- Straightforward site navigation is extremely important for a website.
- Become knowledgeable or hire someone with HTML experience.

- Navigation bars are essential for proper site navigation.

- Cascading style sheets provide formatting and stylistic additions to your web pages.

- Images add visual appeal to your website when used properly.

- Be aware of ADA guidelines concerning accessibility for disabled persons.

- Use *alt*, *height* and *width* tags with images.

- Avoid using frames or create a non-frames version.

Website and HTML resources

The following URLs provide excellent information about the subjects mentioned in this section:

- Castro, Elizabeth (2003) *HTML for the World Wide Web with XHTML and CSS: Visual QuickStart Guide*, 5th edn. Berkeley, CA: Peachpit.

- HTML Goodies: *http://www.htmlgoodies.com*

- HTML Tags: *http://html-tags.info*

- HyperText Markup Language (HTML) home page: *http://www.w3.org/MarkUp*

- Sizzling HTML Jalfrezi: *http://freespace.virgin.net/sizzling .jalfrezi/iniframe.htm*

- Visibone: *http://www.visibone.com*

- World Wide Web Consortium: *http://www.w3.org*

Accessibility resources and ADA compliance utilities

■ The following is an online utility that displays what web pages look like in a text-mode web browser. The site uses the Lynx viewer and is found at the following address: *http://www.delorie.com/web/lynxview.html*

■ The following is another online utility that analyzes web pages and reports problem areas. This site uses Bobby and is found at the following address: *http://bobby .watchfire.com/bobby/html/en/index.jsp*

ADA website

■ More information about ADA guidelines and information can be found at the US Department of Justice ADA home page: *http://www.usdoj.gov/crt/ada/adahom1.htm*

9

Preservation planning

Preservation planning is probably the greatest challenge facing managers of digital collections. No digitization center should ever exclude this course of action when making collections available online, because when a project goes online it is only the beginning of a long-term preservation strategy. We have already discussed some preservation planning in the form of XML, TIFF images, and text documents, but you need to also know why these and other formats are important to you, your collaborators, your projects, your institution, and the people who commission the work. At present, technological advancements in the world are progressing rapidly, and formats change faster than they ever have before. Making sure your older formats can easily make the migration to new formats as they emerge is extremely important. It makes good sense for all of your time, resources, energy, and hard work to be preserved for many years, so taking certain steps to ensure that your projects have a long lifespan is worth the extra effort. We do not know what the future holds, but we must plan for it as best we can. Digital preservation strategies include using standard file formats, migrating and refreshing files regularly, using an archival repository or other reliable offsite storage, choosing appropriate storage media, and ensuring that adequate funding and organizational support are in place.

Standards

Throughout this guide, we have emphasized the importance of adhering to standard file formats. Adherence to standards is essential for long-term preservation of digital objects. When creating your projects, you are actually performing two tasks at once: you are digitizing the actual material for online presentation, and you are preserving the material for long-term archiving. This is accomplished by something known as a *standard*. Standards were developed to ensure the seamless operation of any given product so that it can be interpreted, manipulated, built upon, and recognized by certain protocols that allow users to view, interpret, and use the information that is available to them. If that sounds a little confusing, let us clarify. When a product is developed for consumer use, it must adhere to a standard that is recognized throughout the industry. For example, all TV sets in the US run on the NTSC (National Television System Committee) video standard. All television sets sold in the United States must conform to this standard in order for the viewer to be able to watch TV in the United States. Europe and other countries use different standards such as PAL or SECAM. An NTSC television will not work in a country that uses the PAL or SECAM standard. The same is true for standards in digitization, but in a different way.

Computers can open almost any file format provided you have a program that can successfully open the type of file you have chosen. Much of the material you create requires a certain program that is needed for the editing and creation of files. However, once you convert your archived formats into files for online display, all a person needs is a browser in order to view your online projects. Most people will not have the programs needed to view archived material – that is why you create online viewable formats. Archived formats are generally larger in size than those that are used for online display. In addition, archived formats serve a different purpose than viewable formats. Archived material contains the raw data and preserves the original structure of the documents, while material made for presentation is aesthetically pleasing and in a polished form. It is for these reasons that you must decide which standard or standards you are going to use for your projects.

File formats

Once you have set the standards for your center, it is time to begin creating the files that will ultimately make up your center's collections. File formats provide you with the type of file and format you will be working with and are generally defined by an extension. An extension follows the name of a file and begins with a dot (.) and a series of three or four letters. This identifies what type of file it is and allows you to find out what programs are needed for opening and editing this type of file. For example, a JPEG uses two different extensions: .jpg or .jpeg. The following is an example of how a filename for a JPEG reads using both extensions:

photo.jpg   *or*   photo.jpeg

Both extensions define what type of file it is and what program you must have to open those types of extensions. The Internet also uses two different file extensions to identify web pages: .htm or .html.

File formats provide you with the means to create, edit, convert, and publish your files. Knowing which formats are best suited for your center's digitization purposes and what programs are available to work with your chosen formats allows you to successfully create, archive, and publish collections that will endure and be enjoyed by countless generations for years to come.

Archival file formats preferably will be platform- and software-independent, and non-proprietary. In other words, they will not depend on a particular operating system or software program to be readable, and they will not be the intellectual property of a single company. PDF, for example, is a convenient format for digitizing text files quickly and cheaply, rendering them easy to read and print. However, PDF is a proprietary format of Adobe, and depends on Adobe's software to be displayed. XML and ASCII text files, on the other hand, can be read on PC or Mac operating systems in any text editor. No company owns the intellectual rights to these formats. An ASCII file from 15 years ago is still readable, unlike files in WordStar® or other obsolete word processing formats.

Archival backup/storage

No digitization center should be without a backup system. Computer errors, blackouts, brownouts, hardware failures, software problems and so forth can sometimes cause you to lose data, and the majority of the time the data cannot be retrieved and you must go back and recreate the files from scratch. To avoid such problems, you need to have a disaster recovery plan and determine which method of backup is best suited for your center's needs. The appropriate storage media can mean the difference between accessible digital files and files that have suffered damage and are no longer readable.

Tape backup

There are several methods available for backing up your information. The most common and frequently used is the tape backup method. The tape backup method is an excellent way for you to back up your files on a daily basis because the tapes can easily be written to and erased over a long period of time. Tapes are also an effective means of tracking and monitoring which files were added, deleted or changed since the last time you backed up your drive(s). When you back up a project to a tape, it only backs up the files that were added or changed and deletes any files that were deleted from the server. This provides you with an excellent way to track and monitor your files.

CD/DVD

Another common method used to back up files is to record them to a CD or DVD. Great advancements have been made in optical recording technology over the past few years, and now is the time to benefit from those advancements. As previously discussed in the chapter on hardware, there are many types of DVD and CD media to choose from when deciding to record to disc, so we will not go into that here. (Refer to Chapter 3 for information on the different types of DVD and CD media, as well as the type of recording drive needed to record to those formats.) This section provides a general look at why the use of CD and DVD recordable discs offers you a solution to archiving material, or provides you with supplemental or alternative backup methods.

There is not much difference when recording to a CD or DVD except a DVD holds much more information than a CD. A typical CD holds either 650 MB and/or 74 minutes of audio and music or 700 MB and/or 80 minutes of audio and music. A DVD holds about 4.7 GB of information. CDs and DVDs are ideal for when you want to permanently back up information intermittently. One important aspect of recording to a CD-R and/or a DVD-R is that once the information is recorded to the drive it is permanent and cannot be recorded over. Wear gloves when touching the discs, and keep them in jewel cases or protective archival-quality sleeves in an area with controlled temperature and humidity. Never affix anything to the surface of the disc, or write on any area other than the plastic around the spindle. In addition, it is an excellent idea to keep at least one full copy of the entire contents of your server offsite – preferably in a secure, environmentally controlled location.

Central archival repositories offer promise for the long-term preservation of digital objects. OCLC in the United States has recently started a digital archive that offers secure, top-quality archival storage of digital files for an annual fee based on the number of gigabytes stored. Such professional storage can be affordable for ASCII and XML files that do not require a lot of space but is out of the price range of most institutions for large TIFF files or audio/visual files. There is an emerging ISO standard known as OAIS (Open Archival Information System) that would establish a reference model for a repository responsible for preserving digital information for a designated community. The OAIS standard was originally developed by NASA to manage the digital materials generated by the space program. CEDARS in the UK and NARA in the US use the OAIS standard. More information on OAIS can be found at *http://www.ccsds.org/documents/pdf/CCSDS-650.0-R-2.pdf*.

Migration, refreshing, and emulation

Data *migration* involves keeping digital objects in current file formats. For example, institutions that encoded files in SGML are migrating to XML since it has become the current standard. This can be time-consuming and expensive, so institutions will have to decide when it is time to migrate their files, as they may not be able to update with every upgrade of software. It is of course critical to update before the newer versions of software stop supporting older versions of the files.

Refreshing data means moving it from one medium to another, such as from CD to DVD. This is done to make sure the data is always stored in a medium that is easily readable by current technology. Professors who discover that the only version of their doctoral dissertation is on a 5½-inch floppy disc will testify that it is important to keep track of the media on which your work is stored and to move it before the technology needed to read it becomes obsolete.

Emulation seeks to preserve the usability and functionality of a digital project by using new technology to mimic the way the older technology worked. This is extremely complicated, as everything from the operating system to scripting languages must be emulated, and it is unlikely to be an option for most digital projects.

Metadata

Maintaining a history of the digital object with metadata is a key part of a digital preservation strategy. Administrative metadata, which contains information on the creation, migration, quality control, and rights management of a digital object, is especially important for preservation purposes. Technical information about data capture, file formats, encoding, and provenance will be useful to future managers of the collection. Structural metadata describing the architecture of the digital resources and the relationship between files helps to preserve navigation and presentation of the project. The Metadata Encoding and Transmission Standard (METS) is an XML-encoded metadata format that includes structural and administrative metadata as well as descriptive metadata that identifies the digital object. It can pull together metadata from Dublin Core records and TEI or EAD headers, add further information about an object, and keep it all together in one place. It will likely become the preferred way of managing metadata about digital projects, although it is currently in its infancy.

Ongoing costs

Steven Puglia of the US National Archives and Records Administration estimates that the maintenance costs for digital images will be 50–100 percent of the initial investment for the first ten years, although use of larger centralized repositories might drop this to 10–25 percent (Puglia, 2003). You must remember the ongoing costs of maintenance when planning a digital project and have a plan for funding the preservation of your project. This requires commitment on the part of the institution, because grant funds are not always available for preservation.

Some institutions fund ongoing costs through the sale or licensing of digital images, restriction of access to paying subscribers, or endowment funds. However, an organization should plan for the eventuality that maintenance will become a part of the organization's regular budget. Because of the ongoing costs of maintaining digital collections, organizations will have to decide which collections they can afford to preserve over the long haul. Digital objects that are not being used may have to be sacrificed so heavily used collections can be preserved. There must be organizational policies and procedures in place to assist with such decisions.

Summary and resources

- Digital preservation is a developing field, one that anyone involved in digitization must follow closely.
- For now we can adhere to standards for file formats and storage media, plan for migration and refreshing of data,

keep backup files in an appropriate offsite location, and develop policies and strategies to ensure funding for long-term maintenance.

■ We can also follow developments in the field, such as the National Digital Infrastructure Preservation Program at the Library of Congress, the Digital Preservation Coalition in the UK, and the OAIS standard.

Online resources

■ CEDARS: *http://www.leeds.ac.uk/cedars/*

■ Cornell Online Tutorial on Digital Preservation: *http://www.library.cornell.edu/iris/tutorial/dpm/index.html*

■ D-lib Magazine: *http://www.dlib.org*

■ Digital Preservation Coalition: *http://www.jisc.ac.uk/dner/preservation/prescoalition.html*

■ Library of Congress National Digital Infrastructure Preservation Program: *http://www.digitalpreservation.gov/ndiipp/repor/repor_home.html*

■ The NINCH Guide to Good Practice in the Digital Representation and Management of Cultural Heritage Materials: *http://www.nyu.edu/its/humanities/ninchguide/*

■ OAIS: *http://www.ccsds.org/documents/pdf/CCSDS-650.0-R-2.pdf*

■ OCLC/RLG Preservation Metadata Working Group: *http://www.oclc.org/research/pmwg/*

■ Preservation Management of Digital Materials: A Handbook: *http://www.dpconline.org/graphics/handbook/index.html*

- Preserving Access to Digital Information (PADI): *http:// www.nla.gov.au/padi/*

- Puglia, Steven (2003) *The Cost of Digital Imaging.* Online presentation, 8 August, at: *http://www.rlg.org/ preserve/diginews/diginews3-5.html#feature*

- Report of the RLG Task Force on Archiving of Digital Information: *http://www.rlg.org/ArchTF/*

- UNESCO Guidelines for the Preservation of Digital Heritage: *http://portal.unesco.org/ci/ev.php?URL_ID= 8967&URL_DO=DO_TOPIC&URL_SECTION%3E= 201&reload=1049879672*

Links and resources

The following is a guide to links and other sources of information on digitization.

Accessibility and ADA compliance

- ADA Home Page: *http://www.usdoj.gov/crt/ada/adahom1.htm*
- Bobby™ accessibility testing utility: *http://bobby.watchfire.com/bobby/html/en/index.jsp*
- Lynx viewer: *http://www.delorie.com/web/lynxview.html*

Best practices

- Arts and Humanities Data Service: *http://www.ahds.ac.uk/creating/case-studies/index.htm*
- Berkeley Digital Library SunSITE: *http://sunsite.berkeley.edu*
- Digital Library Federation: *http://www.clir.org/diglib/dlfhomepage.htm*
- IMLS, *A Framework of Guidance for Building Good Digital Collections*: *http://www.imls.gov/pubs/forumframework.htm*

- The NINCH Guide to Good Practice in the Digital Representation and Management of Cultural Heritage Materials: *http://www.nyu.edu/its/humanities/ninchguide*
- Oxford Text Archive Guides to Good Practices: *http://ota.ahds.ac.uk/documents/creating*
- University of Virginia Electronic Text Center: *http://etext.lib.virginia.edu*

Collaboration

- Allen, Nancy and Bishoff, Liz (2002) 'Collaborative digitization: libraries and museums working together', *Advances in Librarianship*, 26: 43–81.
- Arts and Humanities Data Service: *http://ahds.ac.uk/*
- California Digital Library: *http://www.cdlib.org*
- Colorado Digitization Project: *http://www.cdpheritage.org*
- Consortium of Research Libraries CEDARS Project: *http://www.leeds.ac.uk/cedars/*
- Distributed National Electronic Resource: *http://www.jisc.ac.uk/dner/*
- Institute of Museum and Library Services: *http://www.imls.gov*
- National Library of Australia: *http://www.nla.gov.au/padi/*
- National Library of Canada: *http://www.nlc-bnc.ca/*
- National Science Foundation Digital Library Initiative: *http://dli2nsf.gov*

- New Opportunities Fund: *http://www.nof.org.uk/*
- The NINCH Guide to Good Practice in the Digital Representation and Management of Cultural Heritage Materials: *http://www.nyu.edu/its/humanities/ninchguide/*
- Online Archive of California: *http://www.oac.cdlib.org/*
- Schrage, Michael (1995) 'The rules of collaboration', *Forbes ASAP Supplement*, 5 June: 88–9.
- UKOLN: *http://www.ukoln.ac.uk/*

Conferences

- Extreme Markup Languages: *http://www.extrememarkup.com/*
- Internet Librarian International: *http://www.infotoday.com*

Digitization policies

- Digital Library of Georgia Collection Development Policy: *http://dlg.galileo.usg.edu/colldev.html*
- National Library of Australia Digitisation Policy: *http://www.nla.gov.au/policy/digitisation.html*

Encoded archival description

- EAD Help Pages: *http://jefferson.village.virginia.edu/ead/*
- Network Development and MARC Standards Office of the Library of Congress: *http://www.loc.gov/marc/ndmso.html*

Funding

- Arts and Humanities Research Board (AHRB): *http://www .ahrb.ac.uk/*

- Arts and Humanities Data Service (AHDS): information for those applying for AHRB awards: *http://ahds.ac.uk/ ahrb/index.htm*

- Colorado Digitization Program: Funding Resources: *http:// www.cdpheritage.org/resource/funding/rsrc_funding.html*

- Digital Libraries Initiative Phase 2: *http://www.dli2 .nsf.gov/*

- Foundation Center: *http://www.fdncenter.org/*

- Hughes, Lorna (2003) Report on *The Price of Digitization: New Cost Models for Cultural and Education Institutions.* Paper at the Digitization Symposium presented by NINCH and Innodata, New York City, 8 April: *http://www .ninch.org/forum/price.report.html*

- Institute for Museum and Library Services: *http://www .imls.gov*

- Lee, Stuart (2001) 'Digitization: is it worth it?', *Computers in Libraries*, 21(5): 28–32.

- National Endowment for the Humanities: *http://www .neh.gov*

- New Opportunities Fund: *http://www.nof.org.uk/*

- Puglia, Steven (1999) 'The costs of digitization', *RLG DigiNews*, 3(5): *http://www.rlg.org/preserv/diginews*

- Technology Grant News: *http://www.technologygrantnews .com/*

Hardware

- Computers:
  - *http://www.cnet.com*
  - *http://www.dell.com*
  - *http://www.gateway.com*
  - *http://www.pcmag.com*
  - *http://www.pcworld.com*
  - *http://www.zdnet.com*
- Scanners:
  - *http://www.epson.com*
  - *http://www.hp.com*
  - *http://www.microtekusa.com*
  - *http://www.scanstore.com*
  - *http://www.scantips.com*
  - *http://www.umax.com*
  - *http://www.visioneer.com*
- Digital cameras:
  - *http://www.canon.com*
  - *http://www.dcresource.com*
  - *http://www.dcviews.com*
  - *http://www.dpreview.com*
  - *http://www.minolta.com*
  - *http://www.nikon.com*
  - *http://www.olympus.com*

- *http://www.pentax.com*
- *http://www.sony.com*

Metadata

- Dublin Core: *http://dublincore.org*
- METS: *http://www.loc.gov/standards/mets/*

Preservation

- CEDARS: *http://www.leeds.ac.uk/cedars/*
- Cornell Online Tutorial on Digital Preservation: *http://www.library.cornell.edu/iris/tutorial/dpm/index.html*
- D-lib Magazine: *http://www.dlib.org*
- Digital Preservation Coalition: *http://www.jisc.ac.uk/dner/preservation/prescoalition.html*
- Library of Congress National Digital Infrastructure Preservation Program: *http://www.digitalpreservation.gov/ndiipp/repor/repor_home.html*
- The NINCH Guide to Good Practice in the Digital Representation and Management of Cultural Heritage Materials: *http://www.nyu.edu/its/humanities/ninchguide/*
- OAIS: *http://www.ccsds.org/documents/pdf/CCSDS-650.0-R-2.pdf*
- OCLC/RLG Preservation Metadata Working Group: *http://www.oclc.org/research/pmwg/*

- Preservation Management of Digital Materials: A Handbook: *http://www.dpconline.org/graphics/handbook/index.html*
- Preserving Access to Digital Information (PADI): *http://www.nla.gov.au/padi/*
- Report of the RLG Task Force on Archiving of Digital Information: *http://www.rlg.org/ArchTF/*
- UNESCO Guidelines for the Preservation of Digital Heritage: *http://portal.unesco.org/ci/ev.php?URL_ID=8967&URL_DO=DO_TOPIC&URL_SECTION%3E=201&reload=1049879672*

Professional organizations

- American Society for Information Science and Technology: *http://www.asis.org*
- Association for Computing and the Humanities: *http://www.ach.org*
- Society of American Archivists: *http://www.archivists.org*

Selection criteria

- Oklahoma State University Library Electronic Publishing Center: *http://digital.library.okstate.edu/suggest.html*
- Oxford University: *http://www.bodley.ox.ac.uk/scoping/report.html*

Software

- HTML editing programs:
    - Arachnophilia: *http://www.arachnoid.com*
    - Macromedia Dreamweaver: *http://www.macromedia .com/software/dreamweaver*
    - Microsoft FrontPage: *http://www.microsoft.com/ frontpage*
    - Netscape Composer: *http://wp.netscape.com/browsers/ using/newusers/composer*
    - NoteTab Pro: *http://www.notetab.com*
- Imaging programs:
    - Adobe Photoshop: *http://www.adobe.com/products/ photoshop*
    - Jasc Paint Shop Pro: *http://www.jasc.com*
- Page layout programs:
    - Adobe InDesign: *http://www.adobe.com/products/ indesign*
    - Adobe PageMaker: *http://www.adobe.com/products/ pagemaker*
    - QuarkXPress: *http://www.quark.com*
- PDF programs:
    - Adobe Acrobat: *http://www.adobe.com/products/acrobat*
- Text editing/word processing programs:
    - Corel WordPerfect: *http://www.corel.com*
    - Microsoft Notepad: *http://www.microsoft.com*

- Microsoft Word: *http://www.microsoft.com/office/ word*

■ OCR programs:

- OmniPage Pro: *http://www.scansoft.com*

- Prime Recognition: *http://www.primerecognition.com/*

■ Scanning suites:

- ScanSoft PaperPort: *http://www.scansoft.com*

- WOCAR 2.5 is available as a free download at the following URL: *http://tucows.wave.net.br/system/ preview/234813.html*

■ XML editing programs:

- NoteTab Pro: *http://www.notetab.com*

- XML Spy: *http://www.xmlspy.com*

- XmetaL: *http://www.softquad.com*

■ XSLT processors:

- Saxon: *http://saxon.sourceforge.net/*

■ FTP programs:

- WS_FTP: *http://www.ipswitch.com*

■ Freeware and shareware programs:

- *http://www.download.com*

- *http://www.tucows.com*

Standards

■ NISO: *http://www.niso.org*

■ Unicode: *http://www.unicode.org*

Text Encoding Initiative (TEI)

- TEI Consortium: *http://www.tei-c.org*

Training

- Amigos Library Services: *http://www.amigos.org*
- Colorado Digitization Project: *http://www.cdpheritage.org/*
- HATII at the University of Glasgow: *http://www.hatii.arts .gla.ac.uk/*
- Northeast Document Conservation Center School for Scanning: *http://www.nedcc.org/*
- Rare Book School at the University of Virginia: *http:// www.virginia.edu/oldbooks/*
- University College London School of Library, Archives, and Information Studies: *http://www.ucl.ac.uk/admission/ gsp/current/study/depts/art/library.html*
- University of New Brunswick: *http://www.lib.unb.ca/ Texts/*

Tutorials

- Cornell University, *Moving Theory into Practice*: *http:// www.library.cornell.edu/preservation/tutorial/*
- Text Encoding Initiative (TEI) Tutorials and Guides to Local Practice: *http://www.tei-c.org.uk/Tutorials/index.html*

XML

- Harold, Elliotte R. (2001) *The XML Bible*, 2nd edn. New York: Hungry Minds. Available online: *http://metalab .unc.edu/xml/books/bible/*
- XML Cover Pages: *http://www.oasis-open.org/cover/*
- XML for the Humanities: *http://xml.lexilog.org.uk*

XSLT

- Kay, Michael (2001) *XSLT Programmer's Reference*, 2nd edn. Birmingham: Wrox Press.

Website design and HTML

- Castro, Elizabeth (2003) *HTML for the World Wide Web with XHTML and CSS: Visual QuickStart Guide*, 5th edn. Berkeley, CA: Peachpit.
- HyperText Markup Language (HTML) home page: *http://www.w3.org/MarkUp*
- HTML Goodies: *http://www.htmlgoodies.com*
- HTML Tags: *http://html-tags.info*
- Sizzling HTML Jalfrezi: *http://freespace.virgin.net/ sizzling.jalfrezi/iniframe.htm*
- Visibone: *http://www.visibone.com*
- World Wide Web Consortium: *http://www.w3.org*

Glossary

Archival format. A file format that can be expected to be accessible and usable for years to come. Archival formats are generally platform and software independent, non-proprietary, and adhere to certain established standards. TIFF is an example of an archival image file format, and ASCII or XML would be used for archival-quality text files.

Archival imaging. The act of scanning and saving your documents and/or photographs in an image format, usually a TIFF, for long-term storage.

Archiving. The act of preparing paper or electronic documents for long-term storage so the contents are preserved, and can be used, if needed, at a later date.

Audience. Your audience includes any person who views your online material; consider your audience when developing your website to better meet their needs.

Browser. The program you use to look at different sites on the Internet and World Wide Web; examples include Microsoft Explorer and Netscape Navigator.

Cascading style sheet. A file that contains formatting and stylistic information for web pages.

Coding. Using a text editor or markup program to create documents in a markup language such as XML or HTML.

Coding by hand. Using a word processor to create documents in HTML; coding by hand only allows you to view your document when you open it in a browser, whereas markup programs offer more features and versatility.

Collection development policy. See *digitization policy*.

Computer platform. Refers to the type of computer you use, i.e. a PC or Apple Macintosh.

Copyright issues. Permission must be granted from the owner or holder of the copyrighted material before any work can begin on a project.

CSS. See *cascading style sheet*.

Database input. The type and amount of information you save in your database.

Digital collection. A collection of books, papers, photographs, etc. that are digitized and made available in electronic format.

Digital surrogate. The electronic product that results from digitizing the original printed document.

Digitization. The process of converting an image, text, or signal into digital code, usually by scanning or rekeying.

Digitization center. The office or workstation containing the equipment and personnel necessary to perform the digitization process.

Digitization policy. Contains guidelines for access to materials, an analysis of your audience, a plan for preserving original and digital files, a prescription for handling ownership rights issues, a commitment of support for digital projects, and selection criteria for choosing materials to digitize.

Directory structure. The file system you set up for each project, which also provides the navigational framework for the online viewing of that project.

Driver. The operating system calls on the driver to 'drive' a new piece of hardware that has been added to the computer; the driver must be installed in order for the new hardware to work properly.

Driver update. See also *driver*; a newer version of a driver that usually updates and fixes any problems with a piece of hardware.

Editing, text. The process of proofreading and making any necessary changes to the text file in a word processing program after it has been OCR'd so it matches the original document character for character.

Editing, video. The process of transferring video to a computer and using software to edit and produce video files in computer readable formats.

Encoding. Assigning a code to represent data; for digitization, encoding refers to the process of assigning a code to the text, image, and so forth for markup for archiving and online publishing.

File server. A server which houses all the files you create and work with on a daily basis. The file server can be accessed by multiple people at the same time.

File Transfer Protocol (FTP). A protocol used for uploading and downloading files over the Internet.

FTP (File Transfer Protocol). See *File Transfer Protocol.*

FTP client. The FTP client connects to your web server and allows you to create directories and upload your files into the appropriate folder where they can be viewed on the Internet.

GIF (Graphics Interchange Format). GIF files should only be used for online and/or viewing purposes – limited to 256 colors.

Graphics Interchange Format. Also known as GIF; see *GIF*.

Hand coding. See *coding by hand*.

Hardware. The physical components that make up a computer system, e.g. keyboard, mouse, scanner, monitor, hard drive, CD-ROM drive, etc.

Housing. See *digitization center* and *lighting*.

HTML (Hypertext Markup Language). HTML tags are used to build web pages; HTML defines the page layout, fonts, and graphic elements as well as the hypertext links to pages on the website, or to other websites; HTML can be created in text-based editors, WYSIWIG programs, or by hand coding the tags in a word processor.

Hypertext Markup Language (HTML). See *HTML*.

Image editing program. Valuable tool for producing and editing images for archiving and publishing online; these programs allow you to form tasks such as save in multiple formats, resize images, enhance photographs, crop images, create images for your website, and so on.

Image manipulation. Editing an image with a software program that allows you to crop, resize, and make cosmetic enhancements to the image.

Imaging. Working with an image in an electronic format in an image editing program to create an image that is easily viewable and that retains as much of its original attributes as possible while on display on the Internet.

Interface. The means by which the user, hardware, and software interact; user interfaces include the keyboard, mouse, commands, and menus you use to communicate with your computer.

Joint Photographic Experts Group (JPEG or JPG). An image file that displays images in high color but retains a small file size. This file format should only be used for online and/or viewing purposes – it is also the most widely used and accepted image file on the Internet.

JPEG (Joint Photographic Experts Group). See *Joint Photographic Experts Group*.

Lighting. Providing the proper lighting, such as incandescent bulbs, for your digitization center to help prevent mistakes caused by worker fatigue and eyestrain.

Markup. The act of putting text and images in a certain format such as HTML, SGML, or XML by using tags to represent and display the information.

Metadata. Data that describes data; for digitization, the metadata in the document type definition (DTD) describes what data is included in each XML document.

Mission statement. A statement that addresses the goals and purpose of an organization.

Navigation. To move from page to page on the Web or Internet; navigation also includes the ability to move from page to page within a single site.

Navigation bar. Also known as nav bar; a set of links, typically plain text or graphic images, usually in a row or column, that serve as the central point to link you to the key topic areas of a website.

OCR (Optical Character Recognition). The process of converting the text from the archival image into text in the word processor.

Online publishing. Publishing content in a format that is made specifically for viewing over the Internet.

Operating system. The master control program that runs the computer; examples include Microsoft Windows for PCs and Mac OS for Apple computers.

Operations manager. The person who develops the workflow, establishes the standards for each project, determines all organizational details for carrying out the project, prepares the materials for digitization, establishes quality controls, and supervises staff and outsourced vendor relations.

Optical Character Recognition (OCR). See *OCR*.

Outsource. To have work performed by a third-party organization outside of your institution.

Page layout programs. Help you create publications in-house and digitize publications that are in a page layout format; also helpful if you want to create brochures, leaflets, business cards, and so on.

Presentation imaging. Involves taking an archival TIFF image or scanning a new image for the purpose of presentation. An image editing program is used to edit, resize, and save the file as a JPEG for online display.

Preservation. The act of taking preventive measures to ensure that materials will last as long as they possibly can while retaining as much of their original attributes as possible. This includes repairing, housing, and storing the material for several years.

Principal investigator. The person who develops the proposal and evaluation of a project. This includes conducting all planning and providing estimates of equipment and manpower costs. This title to be used if outside funding is sought.

Project. A body of work that has been accepted for digitization purposes.

Project director. The person who develops the proposal and evaluation for the project, conducts all planning, and provides estimates of equipment and manpower costs. This title to be used if no outside funding is sought.

Project participants. The people who perform the physical work of scanning, OCR'ing and markup.

Project phases. Usually defined by the number of steps it takes to complete an entire project. If a project is divided into three phases, the first phase must be completed before work begins on the second phase and the second must be completed before the third.

Proofreading. Checking each letter, number, word, punctuation mark, symbol, and so forth in the text document to be sure it matches exactly with the corresponding character in the printed document.

Proposal. A written document that outlines areas that should be used for consideration when applying for grants and funding for projects.

Quality control. The process of checking and rechecking the quality of work that is performed at all stages of the digitization process to ensure the content is an accurate representation of the original documents.

Quality control procedures. Methods used to ensure that all areas of the digitization process are held to the practices and standards set forth by the center's guidelines.

Rekey. To physically type the contents of a printed material into a word processor.

Rich Text Format (RTF). A text file format that has formatting features much like Word and WordPerfect, but is not as robust as Word or WordPerfect.

Root directory. The main file folder or directory in which all information pertaining to a specific project resides.

RTF (Rich Text Format). See *Rich Text Format.*

Scanning. The act of taking a document or photograph and using a scanner to scan the information into the computer.

SGML (Standard Generalized Markup Language). The original markup language which uses tags to define content information.

Software. A computer program that instructs the computer to perform certain functions.

Spider. An indexing tool for search engines that analyzes web pages from top to bottom in order make information available for online searches.

Tagged Image File Format (TIFF). An image format that is large in size and primarily used for archiving and printing images. The CCITT Group 4 compression scheme is the standard of choice for black and white archival images of text – the TIFF is also used for archiving color images in 24-bit color depth using a lossless compression scheme such as LZW or completely uncompressed.

Tasks. A sequence of events that comprise a complete function.

Text. Short for Plain Text, which is the file format of choice for storing text-based documents using the ASCII standard.

Text-based editors. Programs that allow you to edit or write HTML code; once you write the code with this type of program, you must open your file in a browser to see how the HTML documents will display.

Text editing programs: See also *word processor*; these programs allow you to create, format, and edit text.

Text-only websites. These types of websites do not contain graphics, flash animations, background images, and so forth; a useful form of an ADA-compliant website.

TIFF (Tagged Image File Format). See *Tagged Image File Format*.

Uploading. The act of transferring a file or files from your computer or server to other locations – in this case, from your computer to the web server that is hosting your website.

Usability. How easy something is to use; website usability is extremely important to a project's success when it is published online.

Vision statement. A statement that addresses the vision and hopes of an organization.

Web server. A server that houses files that are used for displaying information on the Internet.

Word Document (.doc). Short for Microsoft Word Document; Microsoft Word allows you to create and edit text more effectively and efficiently than a simple text editor – useful for creating and editing plain text documents; see *text editing programs*.

Word processors. See also *text editing programs*; these programs allow you to create, format, and edit text.

WordPerfect Document (.wpd). A Corel WordPerfect document; Corel WordPerfect allows you to create and edit text more effectively and efficiently than a simple text editor – useful for creating and editing plain text document; see *text editing programs*.

WYSIWYG. An acronym for *What You See Is What You Get*. This is usually referred to with regard to programs that use a graphical user interface to display information. The term comes from how things look on your screen being exactly how they will print and be viewed by others.

XML (Extensible Markup Language). Used for defining data elements in documents and on web pages; it uses a similar tag structure as HTML; however, whereas HTML defines how elements are displayed, XML defines what those elements contain.

XSLT (eXtensible Stylesheet Language Transformations). Computer language used to transform XML documents into other formats, including HTML.

Zoning. The act of selecting an area of text on an image file for OCR purposes.

Index

Valid XML, 91
Validating XML, 91
Video card, 28

Webcounters, 151
Website:
    design, 139
    design, resources, 177
    goals, 139
    layout, 141
    navigation, 139, 143
    publicizing, 150
    statistics, 151
Well-formed XML, 91
Word processor, 53
Workflow, 100
    costs, 125
    log, 101, 102

process, 101
WYSIWYG programs, 49

XML:
    document, requirements, 90
    document, valid, 91
    document, well-formed, 91
    editor, 52
    in libraries, 92
    markup, 88
    parser, 53, 91
    resources, 177
    software, 52
XSLT (eXtensible Stylesheet
        Language Transformations),
        91
    processor, 53